"To be in but not of the world. Drawing on a lifetime of careful study, Gordon T. Smith brings together spiritual theology, sociological analysis, church history, and cultural critique in his new book, *Wisdom from Babylon*. Having apprenticed himself to the church's most trusted teachers whose wisdom still shapes the life and labor of faithful people centuries later, he is at the same time attentive to the contemporary complexity of this task, thoughtfully engaging the tensions of being the church in the globalizing, pluralizing, and secularizing world that is ours. A master teacher whose thinking is marked by unusual clarity and depth, this book is for all who long to make sense of honest faith in the twenty-first century."

Steven Garber, professor of marketplace theology at Regent College and author of *The Seamless Life: A Tapestry of Love and Learning, Worship and Work*

"*Wisdom from Babylon* is a masterful guide for Christian leadership amid the upheavals of our secular age. Global in reach, thick with scholarship, Gordon Smith's work gives us the wherewithal to gain a footing for the journey that besets us. He offers not retreat but presence. This book is hope for anyone asking, 'How can we sing the Lord's song in a foreign land?' (Psalm 137:4)."

David Fitch, B. R. Lindner Chair of Evangelical Theology at Northern Seminary, Chicago, author of *Faithful Presence*

"God is calling the church to a new reality. Of course, the reality of a spiritual community that cuts against the grain of secular liturgy has always existed. We just need to draw upon this ancient wisdom that speaks to us with new intensity. Gordon Smith proposes that we are not merely the church gathered but the church dispersed and present in the world, in particular as lived out in business, education, and the arts. *Wisdom from Babylon* reminds us that we can and should lead from the margins, even as we live as a nonanxious presence in a world full of anxiety. Don't look to this book for techniques and prescriptions. Whether in Babylon or our twenty-first-century world, it's always been about encountering Christ in real time—a reality that is at once deeply profound and highly practical."

Stan Jantz, president and CEO of the Evangelical Christian Publishers Association

"This is a timely book for an age increasing in information yet lacking in wisdom. By exploring diverse streams of Christian thinking, Gordon Smith reveals a deep need to revisit our emerging secular age with fresh eyes. In addition to historical insights, Smith's underlining emphasis reveals that all future leaders will require wisdom shaped by the Scriptures, awakening our courage to lovingly engage with a changing world."

Domenic Ruso, founding church planter of The180 Church in Québec and a faculty member at diverse theological schools across Canada

"*Wisdom from Babylon* is the book of wisdom that is needed for every leader in a Western context. In a moment when people listen to comedians and laugh at politicians, when they are unwavering in their commitment to political ideologies but skeptical of their faith, leaders need a radical reframing of what it means to lead the people of God. Gordon Smith gives us just that: a framework of ancient wisdom translated through practices that every leader can adopt for the present moment. If you're a leader who is feeling lost and reactive, this book serves as a compass pointing us toward the King and the kingdom."

Rick McKinley, lead pastor of Imago Dei Community in Portland, Oregon, and author of *Faith for This Moment*

"I just love how Gordon Smith does theology. His views are evangelical, ecumenical, catholic, orthodox, and justice-hungry, with that wild concoction all put in service to a small but scrappy university in Alberta. We need more leadership like his, informed by theology like his, expressed as lovingly and wisely as this."

Jason Byassee, Butler Chair in Homiletics and Biblical Hermeneutics at Vancouver School of Theology, author of *Surprised by Jesus Again*

WISDOM
FROM
BABYLON

LEADERSHIP *for the*
CHURCH *in a* SECULAR AGE

GORDON T. SMITH

Academic

An imprint of InterVarsity Press
Downers Grove, Illinois

InterVarsity Press
P.O. Box 1400, Downers Grove, IL 60515-1426
ivpress.com
email@ivpress.com

InterVarsity Press® is the book-publishing division of InterVarsity Christian Fellowship/USA®, a movement of students and faculty active on campus at hundreds of universities, colleges, and schools of nursing in the United States of America, and a member movement of the International Fellowship of Evangelical Students. For information about local and regional activities, visit intervarsity.org.

Scripture quotations, unless otherwise noted, are from the New Revised Standard Version of the Bible, copyright 1989 by the Division of Christian Education of the National Council of the Churches of Christ in the USA. Used by permission. All rights reserved.

Cover design and image composite: David Fassett
Interior design: Daniel van Loon
Image: curved paper pieces: © Paul Taylor / Stone / Getty Images

ISBN 978-0-8308-5326-7 (print)
ISBN 978-0-8308-5327-4 (digital)

Printed in the United States of America ∞

InterVarsity Press is committed to ecological stewardship and to the conservation of natural resources in all our operations. This book was printed using sustainably sourced paper.

Library of Congress Cataloging-in-Publication Data
A catalog record for this book is available from the Library of Congress.

P	25	24	23	22	21	20	19	18	17	16	15	14	13	12	11	10	9	8	7	6	5	4	3	2	1
Y	38	37	36	35	34	33	32	31	30	29	28	27	26	25	24	23	22	21	20						

for joella

CONTENTS

Introduction: The Times They Are A-Changin'. *1*

PART 1: READING AND UNDERSTANDING THE TIMES

1   Secularity. *7*
    An Interdisciplinary Consideration

2   Four Contemporary Responses to Secularity, Part 1 . . . .   *22*

3   Wisdom from Babylon *34*
    Attending to the Exilic and Postexilic Prophets

4   Perspective and Wisdom from the Early Church *49*

5   Learning from Historic Minority Churches. *66*

6   Christian Voices from Secular Europe. *80*

7   Four Contemporary Responses to Secularity, Part 2 . . . .   *98*
    The Options Reconsidered

PART 2: FORMING THE ALTERNATIVE COMMUNITY: COMPETENCIES AND DISPOSITIONS

8   Cultivating the Capacity for Liturgical Leadership.   *115*

9   Cultivating the Capacity for Catechetical Leadership *127*

10 Cultivating the Capacity for Missional Leadership *138*

11 Ecumenism in a Secular Age *154*
    A Theological Conviction, a Practical Necessity

12 Cultivating Interiority. *164*
    Spiritual Practice in a Secular Age

Conclusion: Hospitality, the Gospel, and Leadership in a Secular Age *177*

Essential Reading List for Leading the Church in a Secular Age *181*

Name and Subject Index *187*

Scripture Index *191*

INTRODUCTION

THE TIMES THEY ARE A-CHANGIN'

If your time to you
Is worth savin'
Then you better start swimmin'
Or you'll sink like a stone
For the times they are a-changin'.

BOB DYLAN, "THE TIMES THEY ARE A-CHANGIN'"

EFFECTIVE LEADERSHIP FOR THE CHURCH requires the capacity to read the times—to have some understanding of the social, cultural, and economic context in which the church is located. And then, with this insight, it is necessary to cultivate the competencies and dispositions that will provide appropriate guidance for the church in that time and that place.

This means we need to think very intentionally about theological education and formation for leadership to assure that it is consistent with the times—that is, that we are thinking about the ways in which our approach to cultivating leadership equips women and men to lead effectively in the world in which we *actually* live, our circumstances as they present themselves, not as we might wish them to be.

If Bob Dylan is right and "the times they are a-changin'," then it only follows that we ask: What has changed? What do these changes mean? And how do we respond appropriately and effectively? When it comes to the formation of leaders for the church, we must ask about the competencies needed for church leadership—not for a previous time, but for this time. And we must also ask about the spiritual dispositions that we need to cultivate if we are going to provide quality leadership in this particular context.

There are universals, of course. In all times and in all places, there are certain capacities that are inherent in what it means to provide pastoral leadership for the church. We can reflect on the life and mission of the church across cultures and recognize that leadership for the church in both Indonesia and Norway will require certain commitments and capacities, even though the cultural and social context may be very different. It is fruitful to read Martin Luther and Francis de Sales and realize that there are common themes for leadership for the church between the sixteenth, seventeenth, and twenty-first centuries. And yet we need to be particular to our times and to the social, cultural, political, and economic context in which the church is located. This means that we get beyond any nostalgia or wishful thinking. It means that we honestly and courageously engage the world into which we are called, seeking to ask: For this time and this place, what does it mean to provide effective leadership for the church? What are the competencies and dispositions that are needed?

We urgently need qualified, capable, and mature leadership. This does not happen overnight; it takes time, and there are no shortcuts. Speed is rarely a pedagogical virtue. The church in the secular West is facing a very challenging context. It will take time to nurture and cultivate the kind of leadership that can navigate those challenges. Many denominational bodies are facing a dearth of capable leaders for the church, both clergy and lay. Some speak of this as a crisis, and in response there is a propensity to find a quick solution. But nothing is gained, and much is lost, if we do not appreciate that our circumstances are rather complex and that this has significant implications for the formation of leadership.

What follows, then, is meant to provide input for denominational bodies and theological schools who are thinking about leadership formation. But we also need to recognize that, while leaders are taught and mentored and guided, emerging leaders also need to take personal responsibility for their own formation. They cannot be passive; they need to be intentional and self-directed. These emerging leaders will recognize where there are gaps, perhaps in their own formation or in the curriculum of the theological school in which they are enrolled, and they will find what they need wherever it can be found—in an online program from another school or through a short-term continuing education program or through a field experience. Thus what follows also provides a taxonomy for emerging leaders, asking them to consider: If these are the times in which we live, what are the capacities and dispositions that I need to be cultivating? Further, a congregation might ask a similar question. An elders board might work with the pastoral staff to ask if the cohort of pastoral and lay leaders has the requisite capacities and, if not, whether these will be found through training current staff or hiring someone who brings that capacity to the leadership team.

The primary focus of this book is the church in such places as North America, Australia, and New Zealand—those cultures and societies that are in the midst of the shift to a secular society (on the assumption that most of Europe has already made the shift). Much of what I offer here will no doubt be of value to the leadership for the church in other contexts and settings—from Hong Kong and Singapore to Latin America and Africa. But while there are indeed universals, church leaders in each social and cultural context need to ask, for their time and for their place, what it means to provide leadership in their context—even though, of course, we can and must learn from and with one another. In this case, I am asking: What does it mean to provide leadership for the church in an *increasingly* secular context?

PART 1

READING AND UNDERSTANDING THE TIMES

1

SECULARITY

AN INTERDISCIPLINARY CONSIDERATION

I GREW UP IN LATIN AMERICA as the child of missionary parents. Every five years we would take a year back in Canada for what was then called "furlough," a time to reconnect with supporting churches. That meant living for that year in Belleville, Ontario, near my grandmother. There we would attend the Alliance Tabernacle, my mother's home church. Since then, that church building has been sold and the church community now worships in a newer facility on the outskirts of Belleville. The original building is now a mosque and Islamic center.

The university where I serve as president is located in Calgary, Alberta. If you take the light rail from the city center to our campus, the last building you see before you head underground is a mosque. And in Richmond, British Columbia, just south of Vancouver, you can drive along No. 5 Road and see an amazing sequence of buildings: a mosque, a Hindu temple, a Sikh temple, a Jewish learning and community center, a Buddhist temple, and a string of churches.

These are merely indicators that highlight the religious pluralism of Canada. Here Christianity is but one of many religions—perhaps the largest, but still only one of many. What does it mean to be Christian in this pluralist context? And what does leadership for the church look like in such a context?

In addition to religious pluralism, there is another dynamic at play: secularization. In many respects, the growth of a secular mindset is the most significant development of the last fifty to sixty years. *Secularity* does not mean no religion; it means rather that religion is privatized, no longer occupying a privileged voice in the public square. It is different from *secularism*—that is, the assumption in the public square that the default response to any issue or concern is a secular one, whether it be political, economic, or ethical. On the one hand, this means that the state does not endorse any one religious tradition or perspective. But it also means that secularity has become the arbiter of the public square, in effect negating the religious voice. We not only live in a time and place of religious pluralism in Canada, the United States, New Zealand, Australia, and so many other societies (for the moment setting aside Central and Western Europe, who are much further along), but we are also increasingly secular.

Secularity is a highly complex issue, of course. But we need to get some kind of handle on it before we can consider the implications for theological education and leadership formation for the church, so that we are cultivating the kind of church leadership that is needed for this time and in this place.

In this chapter, we will begin to get a read on secularity using an interdisciplinary approach that looks at history, sociology, and philosophy. First, we will consider historical perspectives and how historians document and make sense of the "decline of the church" and the end of Christendom. Second, sociology provides the perspective of those who examine the social and cultural dynamics in which the church is now located. Then philosophers take us to another level, inviting us to look beneath the surface of these developments and giving an additional lens through which to understand our times.

HISTORY AND SECULARIZATION

In the West, notably in Western Europe and those nations whose original settlers came from Western Europe—New Zealand, Australia, Canada, and the United States, for example—each nation was at some point largely Christian. In Europe, this meant a tight link between church and state. But even in the United States, Canada, Australia, and New Zealand, it was assumed that a Christian perspective and ethic shaped the national vision. Christians dominated the political stage, and it was taken for granted that Christian morality would be evident in the nation's legal system.

Students of Christianity in the West consistently point to the 1960s as the significant turning point away from Christendom. While many of the signs of a growing secularization were evident as early as a century prior, this decade—including the late '50s and early '70s—was clearly significant. Callum G. Brown puts it this way: "For the historian of religious decline, there is no period of history as important as the 1960s."[1] He goes on to stress that previous levels of religious decline had been, as he put it, "non-simultaneous, appearing staggered between different nations," but with the 1960s we see a collapse of religious culture as a whole.[2] The contrast or shift in the 1960s was perhaps most dramatic in British culture and British institutions, and Brown makes the point that in the case of Britain at least the change was permanent. Trends were cemented. A century earlier there was an unquestioned consensus regarding what one should believe and how one should live and behave. Anyone who challenged or questioned this was viewed as marginal or even as deviant. By the end of the 1960s, it was almost the reverse: the default religious position became that of the agnostic, at best; religious convictions and perspectives were moved to the margins.

Historian Mark A. Noll is an astute observer of developments in Canada, which he compares to trends in the United States. He noted in 2006 that any semblance of a "Christian Canada" was gone; any reference to God in public documents was at most a concession to a historic legacy. Now the privileged principles that shape the public square are privacy, multiculturalism, tolerance, and public religious neutrality. Religious language was once standard; it is now absent.[3] Church attendance has plummeted, particularly since the 1960s—a benchmark decade in the de-Christianization of Canada. Quebec, once deeply influenced by the church, is now dominated by what Noll calls "secular nationalism"; public symbols and rhetoric are no longer religious but instead represent "a vision of universal multicultural toleration."[4] Tensions between

---

[1]Callum G. Brown, "The Secularization Decade: The 1960s," in *The Decline of Christendom in Western Europe, 1750–2000*, ed. Hugh McLeod and Werner Ustorf (Cambridge: Cambridge University Press, 2003), 29.

[2]Brown, "The Secularization Decade," 29-30.

[3]Mark A. Noll, "Whatever Happened to Christian Canada?," *Church History* 75:2 (June 2006): 247.

[4]Noll, "Whatever Happened," 257.

Catholic (Quebec) and Protestant (English Canada) that defined early Canada are now framed along political and economic lines[5]; any measure of Quebec separatism is now entirely a *secular* aspiration.[6]

What about the United States? Was it a Christian nation that is now increasingly secular? If the answer is "yes," it is often assumed that it is on the same trajectory: Western Europe is secular and Canada increasingly so (though Quebec is remarkably similar to Europe on this score), and now it seems that the United States is also becoming secular such that Canada is at about the halfway point between Europe and the United States.

And yet there are differences. One important point of reference is that the original founders of the United States were unequivocal that theirs was not to be a Christian nation; they insisted on the separation of church and state, saying that no religious expression or entity would be privileged. The aspiration toward life, liberty, and the pursuit of happiness, as expressed in the Declaration of Independence, was hardly a Christian vision—not explicitly so, at least. This was the language of John Locke and the Enlightenment.

And yet religious rhetoric has dominated the national identity and aspirations of the American people. Further, until the 1960s at least, most Americans would have said that their country was and is unequivocally Christian, such that only a person of Christian faith should be the president. It was also assumed that Christian institutions, Christian sacred holidays, and a Christian ethic should continue to guide the national consciousness. That is, there is a strange dual identity to the United States. On the one hand, there is the insistence from the beginning that it is secular, with the formal and even essential-to-American-sensibilities separation of church and state. And, on the other hand, there are voices that persist in calling America a Christian nation. For our purposes, we can ask the question: Is the secularity that was built into the DNA of the United States—the insistence that church and state are separate—becoming more and more evident in public life in the last fifty years? Even if the answer is yes, we still need to acknowledge that just as Europe

---

[5]Noll, "Whatever Happened," 261.
[6]Noll, "Whatever Happened," 264.

and Canada are not monolithic, the same can without doubt be said of the United States: secularism would be more tolerated and affirmed, for example, in Oregon than Alabama.

To answer the question of whether secularity in the United States is increasing, Daniel Cox's 2017 study "America's Changing Religious Identity" is telling.[7] He observes that those who are religiously unaffiliated —that is, those who self-identify as atheist, agnostic, or with no particular affiliation—represent one quarter of all Americans, three times what it was twenty-five years ago. This is predominantly so among younger Americans. The same study confirms what anyone following the news of American elections hears again and again: evangelical Christians— more specifically *white* evangelicals—consistently vote Republican. This voting pattern arises from a conviction that with the Republicans they have a greater chance of keeping America what they have always viewed it to be: a nation under God, evident in a particular moral orientation and with the continued prominence of Christian religious symbols in the public square.

But if the growth of the "nones"—that is, those with no particular religious affiliation—continues in the United States, secularity may well be a definite trend. If so, the United States will follow Western Europe and Canada. Despite government policies that limit Muslim immigrants, for example, this country will become increasingly secular, even if there are pockets—so called Bible belts—where a preponderance of Christians creates its own religious ecozone.

Thus while the establishment clause of the First Amendment is about the neutrality of the state regarding religion, it increasingly means that religion is to be kept out of the public square and that non-religion will be the privileged voice. In 2017, for example, a forty-foot cross in a Washington, DC, suburb was declared unconstitutional. It stands on public land and is a memorial to World War I veterans. The court ruled that "the cross unconstitutionally endorses Christianity and favors Christians." In other words, however much it has been the experience of Americans that Christian faith—including the symbols of Christian faith—are given

---

[7]Daniel Cox and Robert P. Jones, "America's Changing Religious Identity," September 6, 2017, www .prri.org/research/american-religious-landscape-christian-religiously-unaffiliated.

prominence in public spaces, courts in the United States are beginning to apply the establishment clause consistently.

What all of this means for the church in North America, and I am suggesting as well for New Zealand and Australia, is that the Christian voice will no longer be a privileged voice in the public square. We can no longer speak of these countries as "Christian" nations. The dynamics between the United States and Canada are of course different, and historians (including Brown and Noll) stress that there are significant differences. Those leading the church in Quebec are in a rather different cultural context than those who serve the church in Alabama. Yet in both places there is a reality that one and all need to recognize: the rise of secularity, particularly since the benchmark decade of the 1960s.

SOCIOLOGY AND SECULARIZATION

Sociologists who study the phenomenon of religion in the West— beginning with Central and Western Europe and then North America and Australia and New Zealand—consistently observe that religion is in decline in Western societies, and this decline is irreversible. If there are exceptions, they are at most only temporary or, perhaps, aberrations. Any religious affiliation is entirely through voluntary association. Religious influence in the public square is limited at best and, in time, will be nonexistent. Sociologists of religion, in short, observe that Western societies were once highly religious and specifically Christian. Now these societies are increasingly secular.

Joel Thiessen, Canadian sociologist of religion, references the work of Belgian sociologist Karel Dobbelaere, who focuses on Belgium as a kind of core example within Western Europe. Thiessen notes that for Dobbelaere there are three kinds of secularization: societal, organizational, and individual.[8] This trend or development signals that "Christian influence over several other social institutions, such as education, health, or the family gradually diminished, and religion lost its taken-for-granted status in . . . public life."[9] Over time, religion is marginalized; it

---

[8]Joel Thiessen, *The Meaning of Sunday: The Practice of Belief in a Secular Age* (McGill-Queen's University Press, 2015), 14-15.
[9]Thiessen, *The Meaning of Sunday*, 173.

no longer informs the public square. Religious conviction and expression are no longer assumed or even recognized in schools, in the political arena, and in the judicial-legal system. Thus Thiessen notes: "[Peter] Berger and [Steve] Bruce argue that if religion plays a diminishing role in key social institutions it is only a matter of time before individuals look on the world through a lens that does not include much religion."[10]

David Martin offers another perspective. He recognizes the general theory of secularization advanced by Bryan Wilson, Steven Bruce, and Karel Dobbelaere, but he also references such voices as Rodney Stark and William Bainbridge, who speak of the persistent presence and power of religion in societies. Secularity has marked Western Europe, and church participation has dropped off dramatically over a generation—he references France and Holland as primary examples. But Martin is not convinced that this pattern will be followed necessarily in Canada and the United States. He believes that what makes Europe different is that in Europe the church was intertwined with the structures of power. When all the cultural institutions were being challenged starting in the 1960s, the church was included in that challenge: "All the main institutions were subjected to criticism."[11] Rather than the model of secularization seen in Europe, instead Martin sees what we might speak of as the *individualization* of religion: religion becomes nothing more than a personal preference, and the religious communities that flourish are those that emphasize this more consumerist approach to faith.

And yet Martin gives examples of where religion does have a voice and even an influence in politics.[12] In other words, he is not convinced that there is "a single [secularization] track to a common terminus."[13] Having said that, Martin does not doubt that there are substantial changes afoot. His points of comparison are intriguing; for example, he notes, "Throughout Western Europe the secularizing process has accelerated since the 1960s . . . even above all in the mainstream churches."[14]

---

[10]Thiessen, *The Meaning of Sunday*, 15.

[11]David Martin, *On Secularization: Towards a Revised General Theory* (Aldershot: Ashgate, 2005), 23.

[12]Martin, *On Secularization*, 24.

[13]Martin, *On Secularization*, 47.

[14]Martin, *On Secularization*, 87.

But again he insists there is not a set pattern or trajectory; secularity looks very different in different contexts. Thus, for example, Martin contrasts Scandinavia and Britain, noting that while they are similar in terms of the level of religious practice, Scandinavia ranks low on practice but high on formal identification with the church. By contrast, Britain is low on "belonging" but a higher percentage of British people affirm that they believe. Thus, "Britons believe without belonging while Scandinavians belong without believing."[15] Then also, Martin acknowledges that in Catholic societies there is significant evidence that Catholic Christians recognize and affirm the pope and other religious leaders, but even when there is a strong Catholic identity such as in Poland and Ireland, this "does not imply recognition of ecclesiastical authority or a desire for its embodiment in secular law."[16]

In other words, while secularization theory—the idea of an irreversible trajectory—can be challenged, secularity is still the cultural context for the church, even though it may look very different in different settings. The cultural and social dynamics of Western Europe, North America, Australia, and New Zealand have changed in fundamental ways. We live in a different world—with a different set of dispositions, defaults, and assumptions.

It is no surprise that this will not look the same in every context and setting. Further, it is important to stress that this does not mean that religious expression cannot flourish. It merely means that with secularization religious people cannot look to society for reinforcement of their personal religious identity and sensibilities. Religious expression can still flourish as long as the church and the individual are attentive to the changing social and cultural dynamic and then intentional in that response.

In light of all this, we need to ask: Is secularization a master narrative? That is, can we genuinely speak of it as a trend? If so, just as Britain and Europe are increasingly secular, it is just a matter of time before the same will happen in the United States, with perhaps New Zealand, Australia, and Canada further along on the secularization trajectory. If it is a master

---

[15]Martin, *On Secularization*, 86.
[16]Martin, *On Secularization*, 87.

narrative, this does not mean religious expression has declined. There is not necessarily less religious experience; there might even be more religious activity. Rather, what is meant is this: secularity is now the default mode in the public square. Secularity speaks not so much of the decline of religion as that religious faith no longer has a privileged voice within a society. It is for this reality that we are being called to be the church and to provide leadership for the church.

We will look at this in more detail in the chapters to follow, considering the diverse ways in which the church and Christians have chosen to respond. But first we need to consider the response to secularization that comes from the discipline of philosophy.

PHILOSOPHY AND SECULARIZATION

There are many voices that consider the phenomenon of secularization through the lens of the ancient discipline of philosophy—asking about the meaning of life and doing the work of making sense of our lives and our situations while fostering our capacity for wisdom and understanding. I will mention two: the older Catholic Louis Dupré, professor emeritus at Yale University, and the younger Reformed Protestant James K. A. Smith, notably in his interactions with the philosopher Charles Taylor.

Dupré's most cogent contribution to the conversation about secularization is his attention to the religious impulse that cannot be suppressed or sublimated. In his *Transcendent Selfhood: The Loss and Rediscovery of the Inner Life*, he insists that there is within each human person a longing for transcendence. He refers to the opening of Augustine's *Confessions* and that great line, "You have made us for yourself, and our heart is restless until it rests in you."[17] Dupré insists that with secularization this sense of the transcendent is not lost; indeed, it cannot be lost because this impulse is too integral to human identity to ultimately be suppressed. However, it is obscured by what Dupré calls "the inward turn."[18] Religion becomes a private affair: "In a secularized society the religious

---

[17]Louis Dupré, *Transcendent Selfhood: The Loss and Rediscovery of the Inner Life* (New York: Seabury, 1976).
[18]Dupré, *Transcendent Selfhood*, 26.

person has nowhere to turn but inward."[19] He observes that "the center of human piety has moved from a shared and community oriented faith to a personal, expressive, indeed inward orientation where the self encounters its own transcendence. The modern believer sacralizes from within a world that no longer possesses a sacred voice of its own."[20] Thus he concludes:

> While in the past nature, verbal revelation, and ecclesiastical institutions determined the inner experience, today it is mostly the inner experience which determines whether and to what extent outer symbols will be accepted. The religious person embraces only those doctrines which cast light upon his inner awareness, joins only those groups to which he feels moved from within, and performs only those acts which express his self-transcendence.[21]

Thus, if I am reading Dupré correctly, spirituality is not gone; there is no less of a religious impulse or longing. Rather, it has become *personal-expressive*: individual, internal, and subjective. Of course, the good news for those who care about religion is that there remains an affirmation of the interior life—the mystical dimension—the reality that the essence of religious experience is located in the interior human consciousness. A nominal or merely formal religious identity will be less and less likely to be the norm. People will as a rule only participate in religious activities if there is meaning for them in these activities. They will not be going through the motions or merely attending church as a cultural norm. Religious expression will be more authentic.

But there is also not-so-good news. This orientation toward the personal, subjective, and interior is not sustainable. We cannot in the end be spiritual without being religious. Authentic spirituality needs the sustaining power of a community with a shared faith, conviction, orientation, and accountability. Religious belief is inherently communal.

The other bit of not-so-good news is captured by a phrase from Gregory Baum in an essay on secular Quebec. In it, he speaks of "an

---

[19]Dupré, *Transcendent Selfhood*, 27.
[20]Dupré, *Transcendent Selfhood*, 29.
[21]Dupré, *Transcendent Selfhood*, 30-31.

unexpected secularization of personal consciousness."[22] This is where the magisterial work of Charles Taylor is so significant.[23] In *A Secular Age*, Taylor speaks not so much of the decline of church attendance or the ways in which religious influence has waned in the West. Rather, what we learn is that secularity is a different *consciousness*. There is a secular way of being—of thinking, seeing, feeling, and acting. It is not merely that there is less religion, and not merely that now religion is marginal—that Christianity and the church no longer have a privileged voice. It is that secularity has become a way by which the world is seen and engaged.

I am going to engage Taylor through the lens of James K. A. Smith, notably through his *How (Not) to Be Secular: Reading Charles Taylor*. Smith has provided us with an accessible and insightful read of Taylor and effectively sets up our agenda here: to ask what it means to provide leadership for the church in a secular age. As Smith notes, Taylor recognizes the way in which the social, cultural, and religious landscape has changed, speaking of the massive shift from a world where the default assumption was some form of belief to the default assumption now of unbelief or the lack of belief.[24] In this, Smith—building on and interpreting Taylor—seeks to highlight something that must be attended to. It is not so much that there is secularity "out there" as that we are *all* secular. That is, unwittingly we have drunk the water and breathed the air; rather than Christianity maintaining a presence in a secular society, secularity has infiltrated the church.

In this way of thinking, the Christian faith is being lived out in an essentially secular way. Yes, Taylor acknowledges that we live now in a pluralistic context and setting. And yes, the sociologists and the historians are right that secularity is now the default perspective within these societies. But what Taylor is saying is that this has also changed the way

---

[22]"Catholicism and Secularization in Quebec," in *Rethinking Church, State and Modernity: Canada between Europe and the USA*, ed. David Lyon and Marguerite Van Die (Toronto: University of Toronto Press, 2000), 196 (quoted by Mark Noll in "Whatever Happened," 270).

[23]Charles Taylor, *A Secular Age* (Cambridge, MA: The Belknap Press of Harvard University Press, 2007).

[24]James K. A. Smith, *How (Not) to Be Secular: Reading Charles Taylor* (Grand Rapids, MI: Eerdmans, 2014), 18-19.

that the faith is being lived. And it is in this context that Smith, in response to Taylor, is asking the necessary questions: What does belief look like now? How is the faith communicated and taught? And, How does faith formation happen—for this generation?[25]

In the remainder of this section, I will highlight two things that emerge from Taylor and Smith. More could be said, but at the very least these two realities need to be identified.

Disenchantment. Taylor notes that we now live in a world that has lost a sense of transcendence. We live in a world of immanence; everything that counts and matters is what we see and feel and touch. Human flourishing is defined entirely in mundane terms.

Smith notes that this immanent frame "both boxes in *and* boxes out, encloses and focuses." And for many, this frame is impenetrable.[26] Some live in an entirely closed immanent frame—what Taylor calls "closed world structures." We have changed from a social context in which the default was religious faith and identity to a social context where belief is the exception and not the norm. And yet Taylor and Smith—like Dupré—insist that we are haunted by transcendence; secularity and secularism cannot ultimately squelch the longing for more than mere materiality. For Taylor, the catalysts for this sense of transcendence are beauty, death, and moral obligation. These are simply inescapable in the human consciousness; there is within each person a longing for more, a longing for meaning and purpose. N. T. Wright speaks in similar fashion when he says even the most secular people have within them a longing for spirituality, a hunger for relationship, and a yearning for beauty.[27]

Two things must be noted in this regard. First, conversion is as much as anything about at some point being open to the possibility of transcendence. And second, those who do believe do not believe uncritically; they have chosen to believe in the face of negative odds. This means that Christian faith—indeed, all faith—has to now be intentional and

---

[25]Smith, *How (Not) to Be Secular*, 23.
[26]Smith, *How (Not) to Be Secular*, 92.
[27]N. T. Wright, *Surprised by Hope: Rethinking Heaven, the Resurrection, and the Mission of the Church* (New York: HarperOne, 2008).

thoughtful. The default mode in our societies is immanence, not transcendence; and thus those who believe are going against the grain.

In working against this disenchantment, we might consider the way that time is perceived and also reference the artists in our midst. It is a sign of secularity that we are inclined to view time in linear terms, as something that can be controlled and managed. In a secular universe, days have no particular meaning other than as "space" to get things done. As part of our Christian formation, we might ask how we communicate a sacred perspective on time. We also need to value the work of artists, especially poets. The genius of these poets is that faith is not reduced to mere morality. One cannot but recognize the extraordinary role that the poetry of George Herbert played in the conversion experience of Simone Weil, for example.[28]

If conversion and belief mean that we must first come to some measure of acceptance that there is indeed another sphere of reality, we must speak of "thin places" where the intersection between the two spheres of reality are remarkably close. Might it be that awareness of these spaces is more vital and essential and necessary that ever before?

The buffered self. Second, in speaking of a "secular age" we must refer to the mechanism for living or surviving in this context—what Taylor calls "the buffered self." In this secular age we are no longer truly connected, either to others or to ourselves. If we are to have a sense of transcendence, we necessarily need to belong. We cannot know and embrace transcendence if we are isolated and insulated from the world around us. We need to find a faith that is grounded and expressed in community. We cannot hope to encounter transcendence if we are nothing but spiritual monads.[29]

But more, one of the deep marks of our age is that any spirituality that we might have is self-constructed: we create our own meaning and follow our own inspiration. Tolerance means that we let each one "affirm their own way." This view of the world is summarized in the apt phrase "expressive individualism."[30] In this context, there is only one authority: the

---

[28]In chapter 8 I will highlight both the importance of the church calendar and the crucial place that artists occupy in the life and mission of the church.

[29]Smith, *How (Not) to Be Secular*, 30.

[30]Smith, *How (Not) to Be Secular*, 88.

authority of one's self as the ultimate arbiter of one's life and existence. The challenge for the church is to locate authentic spirituality within an authoritative community that has the capacity to foster a true sense of meaning and transcendence.

CONCLUSION

Emerging leaders for the church in a culture and society that is increasingly secular should be reading historians, sociologists, and philosophers who have wrestled with secularization. In so doing, several questions will emerge: Can the church survive—and more, actually *thrive*—in this context? Can we speak of vibrant Christian communities in this time and place? Can we flourish as individual Christian believers? What does Christian witness look like, and what might this mean for the way in which we engage the practices of evangelism, Christian initiation, spiritual formation, and liturgy? What does Christian mission look and feel like in such a time? And, bottom line: What does leadership for the church look like? What are the key capacities and dispositions needed for leadership in the church for a secular age?

We ask these questions recognizing three dangers or temptations that we might face as a Christian community. The first is that with secularization, religion is privatized and becomes little more than a personal, subjective, and individual experience. One of the perhaps unintended consequences of the marginalization of religion is that people tend to approach religion in a consumerist manner, asking if it meets our felt needs and believing that what works for one person might be different than what works for another. Further, some sociologists have noted that with the secularization process, more subjective forms of Christian spirituality seem to actually thrive. By *subjective*, I mean an emphasis on interior experience—perhaps a very intense personal experience of the "Spirit" or the spiritual—at the expense of a spirituality of genuine engagement with the world. It is a spirituality that, ironically, actually reinforces the secular agenda by being personal and interior and subjective.

Alongside the danger of subjective escapism is the propensity to fight. When religion does go public in a secular age, it does so in an adversarial manner, eager to "win our country back."[31] The danger here is that the church is forced into a posture of constantly being at war with its social and cultural context. This adversarial posture also potentially becomes focused toward other religious groups. Those who are "antisecular" are, as often as not, praying that the "house of Islam" will fall, and thus equating the threat of secularism with the threat of Islam. In this, they fail to discern—and are indeed blind to—how the call to Christian witness has changed in an increasingly pluralist context.

Finally, we are in danger of not recognizing how secularity has become second nature to the society at large and thus so easily to the church as well. We do not realize how secular we have become in the patterns of our shared life, worship, and mission, and in the assumptions that shape what it means for us to be the church.

---

[31]In the words of the popular Christian worship song from Rend Collective, "Build Your Kingdom Here" (2012).

2

FOUR CONTEMPORARY RESPONSES TO SECULARITY, PART 1

BEFORE WE ADDRESS THE QUESTION of how we ought to think about what it means to be the church in a secular age, and what implications this might have for the way in which leadership is cultivated, it is helpful to observe that not all Christians respond to secularity in the same way. Naming the responses and identifying which actually make the most sense will help us to frame the question of leadership and the competencies needed for leadership in this context.

There has always been a diversity of responses to the social, cultural, political, and religious context in which the church has found itself. One of the most defining and seminal publications to demonstrate this was H. Richard Niebuhr's *Christ and Culture*, published in 1951.[1] Niebuhr argued that it is helpful to think in terms of five distinctive responses—each of which, he noted, had historical precedent.

For the first response, "Christ against Culture," Niebuhr used the example of the early church father Tertullian, along with more contemporary perspectives like the Mennonites. These have postured their faith in terms of a *rejection* of human culture and systems. The emphasis is on discontinuity between the culture and the Christian faith. With the second, "Christ of Culture," Niebuhr identified a contrasting perspective that emphasized continuity, rather than discontinuity, with the culture. Christ in this case *fulfills* the aspirations and longings of human society. This was Niebuhr's observation regarding Protestant liberalism: all it did was confirm culture rather than challenge and truly redeem it. "Christ

---

[1]H. Richard Niebuhr, *Christ and Culture* (New York: Harper & Row, 1951).

Above Culture" is the perspective that calls the church to be bilingual and "bi-cultural," speaking to the need to be fully present to our society and culture but also have a distinctive religious or Christian identity. Niebuhr noted that the danger here is that the church would live in two bifurcated zones, never truly inhabiting either or seeing the points of deep connection between them. "Christ and Culture in Paradox" is a posture that emphasizes constant tension, even conflict, between culture and faith. And finally, "Christ the Transformer of Culture" has a vision of cultural redemption: that all aspects of human life, society, and culture could be infused with a Christian vision of human flourishing. This perspective assumes that the created order is good, and that thus culture and human society are redeemable.

Part of what made Niebuhr's book so interesting was that for each of these views, he identified a church father or a Reformer or both who advocated for it. Though he clearly himself leaned toward the last view, he recognized that in certain times and seasons all five of these might have viability.

I want to suggest that in our own day there are four distinct responses to the phenomenon of secularity. These are not meant as a parallel to Niebuhr; rather, inspired or encouraged by Niebuhr, I want to describe how it appears that Christians, churches, and Christian institutions are choosing to respond to the rise of secularity.

The focus of this chapter, then, is describing these four responses to secularity. Each of the next four chapters will speak to a source of wisdom for how we might make sense of these four responses. Then in chapter 7 I will come back to these four responses and reconsider them in light of the insights that have emerged.

OPTION A: THE "GO ALONG TO GET ALONG" RESPONSE

In many respects, the most common response of Christians—particularly in North America—is to accept that they now live in a secular context and to live essentially a bifurcated way of life, occupying two ways of being that are kept separate. In the one, at home and within the context of Sunday worship and church activities, they are Christians. And Monday through Friday, they are essentially no different in their approach to life and work than their secular neighbors. The church essentially functions as a placeholder for religious sensibilities; it is a place to come away from the world and culture and be in a Christian zone. But the church itself has little if any orientation to the world.

Secular voices essentially demand this. They are willing to tolerate religion as long as it is kept private and out of the public square, and many Christians go along. Their religious identity or faith is private and thus siloed from their life and work outside of home and their church community. They choose to lie low, blend in, and accept that their Christian identity has at most a marginal impact on how they live their lives and how they engage their vocations in the world. Their approach to business, for example, would be no different from that of a non-Christian colleague or neighbor—meaning not that they are dishonest, but rather that civility and good approaches to doing business are as much about cultural norms as they are about faith informing their work.

When it comes to the culture around them, Christians with this approach accept that society is changing and choose to see this as "just the way things are." They also are inclined to think that there is little or nothing to be gained by fighting secularism. Some may actually see it as better than what they view as the alternative—religious fundamentalism. They view their faith as very real, but it is best kept private and personal. They accept the secular assumption that religion is tolerated as long as it does not seek to have a voice in the public square. For an individual Christian, the message is simple: "You are free to be a Christian, of course; we have religious freedom in this country. But leave your religion at home when you go to school or work."

This also finds expression on an institutional level. There are universities, for example, that may well have a distinct religious identity. In a Catholic context, it is even possible that the university would be a diocesan college or university. But, as one president of such an institution put it to me, even though they have a deeply Catholic history and identity, there is a "firewall" between the theology faculty and the rest of the university curriculum. Outside of courses in religion and theology, one would not know the difference between this university and a public university or one with no particular religious identity. Again, a secular society is quite content with this: the religious identity of the university is acceptable only if it is part of its historic legacy and does not influence the way it actually does higher education.

For many Christians—indeed, it may be the majority of Christians in North America—this approach to secularity works fine for them. The question, of course, is whether this is consistent with the call of Christ to the church to be salt and light, an instrument of God's grace, within the world. For those with an eschatology that is only about ultimate escape from the world, with a minimal notion of "being saved," this might be a viable option. They might even be encouraged that their churches are growing in terms of Sunday attendance. But for those who believe that the church is called to be in the world, this approach raises serious questions.

Having said that, we do need to ask: If secularity is our new reality, are there ways in which the church might be called to just "go along to get along"? Are there developments that we might well accept and just let be?

OPTION B: THE MONASTIC RESPONSE

A second response to secularity could be called *monastic retreat*. This is not a new phenomenon, of course; some in the church have responded this way in almost every generation: retreating from society and building a protective wall between it and the Christian community of faith. Sometimes it has been a literal wall, as in the case of cloistered monastic communities. But as often as not it is a sociological wall—reflecting a sharp discontinuity that may or may not include physical separation.

Think here of the desert fathers or the Benedictine monastic movement, but also of the more contemporary communities like the Amish that establish alternative rather than integrated societies. This might also reflect something of the vision of the Bible school movement, which still has institutions that choose to be "apart"— intentionally creating spaces or venues that protect young people by shielding them from the city. In other words, some still choose the monastic alternative in response to the society in which they find themselves.

It is fascinating to follow the discussion about whether monasticism "saved" not only the church but civilization. Such is the argument, for example, of Thomas Cahill in his *How the Irish Saved Civilization*.[2] And yes, a case can be made that the monastic houses preserved ancient learning. Morris Berman references the work of David Knowles, who documented how monasteries "became centers of light and life in a simple, static, semi-barbarian world, preserving and later diffusing what remained of ancient culture and spirituality."[3] Berman then goes on to speak of "the monastic option in the twenty-first century." His concern is the decline of American democratic institutions and the healthy middle class rather than the decline of Christian faith per se, but he raises the question: Is retreat a legitimate approach to the "decline" of civilization?

A similar argument is made by Rod Dreher in his *The Benedict Option*.[4] He makes the case for what some speak of as the "new monasticism," resurrecting or restoring some of the ancient Benedictine principles of common life. His contention is that we are living in a world marked by cultural decline, and that churches are "largely ineffective in combating the forces of cultural decline."[5] In his mind, the "culture wars" approach—which I will summarize below as option C—has not worked; we are no more than "chaplains" to a consumerist culture. He calls the church to be countercultural and to avoid all compromise, regardless of cost. The only way forward, the only way to not only survive but thrive, is to organize and be governed as *monastic* communities.

Dreher's use of the word *chaplains* is unfortunate; he clearly does not realize that chaplains may well be vanguards of Christian witness in a secular society. But without being distracted by that aside, consider the merits of his proposal. He is not calling for gender-specific communities but rather a kind of "Christian village" where families and communities pass on the faith from one generation to the next. The idea is

---

[2]Thomas Cahill, *How the Irish Saved Civilization: The Untold Story of Ireland's Heroic Role from the Fall of Rome to the Rise of Medieval Europe* (New York: Doubleday, 1995).

[3]Morris Berman, *The Twilight of American Culture* (New York: W. W. Norton, 2000), 78.

[4]Rod Dreher, *The Benedict Option: A Strategy for Christians Living in a Post Christian Nation* (New York: Sentinel, 2017).

[5]Dreher, *Benedict Option*, 1.

that Christians would live in intentional community, in close proximity. Church would not be framed as a consumerist experience for those who want to commute to their worship service of choice; rather, being the church would be a life of commitment—of community with mutual accountability.

Dreher's assumption is that the world and the culture have gone from bad to worse—thus the motif of decline. Secularity is in his mind an unparalleled bad thing; the church has lost the battle for the West. Now, therefore, is the time for retreat and retrenchment.

Here the question arises much like it does for the "go along to get along" alternative: Does this approach provide a sufficient level of engagement with the world so that the church is truly salt and light? Is the decline motif more alarming than necessary? Is retreat truly the only option? Even if the answer is no, might there be wisdom here? Are there monastic principles and practices that do have relevance and applicability for Christians who live in a post-Christian secular context?

OPTION C: THE CULTURE WARS RESPONSE

Then there is what has been called the "culture wars" response to secularism. The assumption here is that society was once Christian and that this needs to be restored. Christian perspectives and values were once privileged, and the task now is to turn the clock back and recover that voice and position in society.

As discussed in chapter 1, there is a debate over whether the United States was ever Christian or even was intended to be Christian. Regardless, those of the culture wars persuasion are convinced that, even if there was something in the founding documents of the United States that separated church and state, nevertheless the country is at its best when Christian values and Christian leaders shape the culture. Thus, they fight to keep the nation Christian.

The "war" in "culture wars" is highly politicized, with certain political parties viewed as more favorable to Christian or biblical values. The war is typically fought on three fronts: in the courts, at educational institutions, and in the legislatures. Culture-war Christians are in a battle to preserve and sustain Christian values and commitments—typically spoken of as "biblical values"—and their commitment is to find a way for these values to shape judicial decisions, inform the school curriculum, and influence laws.

As often as not, there are also two "fronts" to this war. The one is against secularity itself. The other is against additional or related threats, or perceived threats, such as Islam. As one book advertisement in a Christian magazine put it: "Our Way of Life Is Under Attack." The book in question unites the two fronts in its subtitle: "Aggressive Secularism, Radical Islam, and the Fight for our Future."[6] In other words, those who make the case for the church to be "at war" often link secularity and the more ancient adversary, Islam. Many speak of Islam as the great global threat to the church, and claim that this is increasingly a threat in the West.

Frances FitzGerald gives a powerful overview of the culture wars response to secularity in her remarkable *The Evangelicals: The Struggle to Shape America*.[7] She provides a very thorough and engaging history of evangelicalism going back to the Great Awakenings through the twentieth century up until the present and notes how, starting in the 1960s, evangelicals became increasingly politicized. This is journalism at its best, narrating—with minimal commentary and interpretation, often in their own words—the responses and reactions of evangelical leaders and spokespersons to the changing character of American society and culture.

Perhaps it was the election of the first Roman Catholic president. Perhaps it was the US Supreme Court decisions in 1962 and 1963 to ban prayer and Bible reading in public schools, or the action of the Congress to pass two civil rights acts that granted the full rights of citizenship to African Americans. Or it may have been the Supreme Court legalization of abortion in 1974 with *Roe v. Wade*. For many, it is the parallel issue of human sexuality that is the most dire consequence of living in a secular age: the challenge to what is perceived to be the very core of human identity—sexuality as male and female and marriage as exclusively between one man and one woman.

---

[6]Michael Youssef, *The Hidden Enemy: Aggressive Secularism, Radical Islam, and the Fight for Our Future* (Carol Stream, IL: Tyndale Momentum, 2018).

[7]Frances FitzGerald, *The Evangelicals: The Struggle to Shape America* (New York: Simon & Schuster, 2017).

Whatever the catalyst or catalysts, evangelical leaders emerged for whom all of this meant "war": evident, notably, with the election of Richard Nixon in 1968 and then doubly so with Ronald Reagan in 1980. The conservative evangelical wing of the church found its voice and its influence and its identity within the Republican Party. Evangelicalism then and now is certainly not monolithic, but voices like Ron Sider and Jim Wallis and David Moberg, with their commitment to an evangelical social gospel, tended to be the minority voice. Increasingly, Jerry Falwell and Pat Robertson dominated the headlines.

Twenty years later, the key players have changed but the tone is similar. This is "war," and the battle lines are drawn over abortion rights and questions of human sexuality. The battle ground is the Congress, the presidency, and, ultimately, the judiciary. And the vehicle to win this war is the Republican Party. Tied up in all of this is advocacy for Israel, support for gun rights, opposition to environmental protections, and deep antipathy to Islam. Evangelical support for Donald Trump in 2016 and beyond was all based on the assumption that he could deliver for them on these fronts in the culture war. While principally an American response to secularism, this perspective does spill over to other countries: witness Franklin Graham's visit to Canada in 2017 as he denounced secularism and Islam together.

As FitzGerald notes, not all who might identify themselves as evangelical have chosen the culture wars posture in their response to secularity. She mentions, for example, Greg Boyd, Jim Wallis, and Jimmy Carter. And yet, for good or ill, the assumption has often been made that this is the response of the majority of those who would self-identify as evangelical.

When evaluating this option, one has to ask: Is it working? Does the unqualified support of political candidates actually preserve the culture as a Christian culture? Or does something else get compromised? Does the "culture wars" approach reflect the best way for the church to engage both the limits and the potential of living and working in a secular context?

However, as we have asked of the first two options, might there also be wisdom here? Is there something for which the church does, indeed, need to fight? Are there values and commitments that need to be defended—in the legislatures, the courts, and the educational system? If so—if we are to have "a hill we are willing to die on"—what issue or issues *should* shape the political agenda of the church?

OPTION D: THE RESPONSE OF "FAITHFUL PRESENCE"

There is also a fourth response to secularity that has been described as "faithful presence." The name comes from James Davison Hunter's *To Change the World: The Irony, Tragedy, and Possibility of Christianity in the Late Modern World;*[8] see also David E. Fitch's book by that title.[9]

Hunter and Fitch suggest that the culture wars approach does not work; it creates an adversarial posture toward society at large that in the end undercuts the potential for the church to be an instrument of transformative change. Rather than seeking to leverage power within political systems as the means to preserve certain values, instead Christians should accept that this new reality presents an *opportunity*. The church can and must not only accept but embrace this situation and then, from this posture of acceptance, fashion a way of being present to and engaged with society in a manner that is both faithful to the gospel but also transformative.

For Hunter and Fitch, it is imperative that we think in terms of the long arc of history and realize that true leverage within a society is exerted from a place of being present—humbly and charitably—and participating in the defining institutions of our culture. We are deeply and fully Christian, but *within* society rather than at war with society. We do not need to panic or bemoan our state; we can intentionally leverage the openings and inflection points that are given to us precisely because we live in a secular age.

This vision of faithful presence assumes, as a fundamental theological conviction, that God is present in the world. The lack of Christian voices or presence, and the fact that a society is increasingly secular, does not imply that God is not present. The presence of God and the grace of God in the world give us a different set of lenses through which to see and

---

[8]James Davison Hunter, *To Change the World: The Irony, Tragedy, and Possibility of Christianity in the Late Modern World* (Oxford: Oxford University Press, 2010).
[9]David E. Fitch, *Faithful Presence: Seven Disciplines that Shape the Church for Mission* (Downers Grove, IL: InterVarsity Press, 2016).

engage with the society around us. We do not bifurcate as Christian and non-Christian, religious and secular, light and dark, on the assumption that everything outside of the immediate domain of the church is dark, somehow demonic, and an inherent threat to the gospel and to God.

While Hunter provides a theological and philosophical vision for being present in and to the world, Fitch builds on this vision and speaks of specific practices. Without the practices, the idea of faithful presence is just a good idea. But the fundamental vision or principle remains the same: God is in our world, and we need to recognize and not underestimate the way in which the presence of the church and of Christians within the social fabric of institutions is transformative.

I serve as the president of a university that has a post-baccalaureate two-year education degree program that equips women and men to be teachers within the public school system. As I do my work, I try to imagine what it might mean to be the only Christian in a public school. It reminds me that we are not called to merely "go along to get along," that we should be very present to the city and not choose to withdraw to a specifically Christian (monastic) community, and that the Christian is definitely not at war with the public school system (which would be a useless battle with little if anything gained). Rather, Hunter and Fitch provide these teachers an appreciation for how their presence in the school system must not be underestimated. It can be transformative.

How might we respond to option D, the approach of faithful presence? I suggest two things, for now—with more commentary to come in chapter 7. First, similar to option A, this option also accepts secularity as the new dynamic to which the church is called. Rather than either fighting or being resigned to secularism, this option suggests that we look at new ways or new opportunities for Christian witness that may emerge in a secular context.

However, second, we do need to ask: Can faithful presence, on its own, sustain the dynamic of our calling in the world? Fitch, in speaking of practices, moves the conversation forward. If the church is to be present to and in the world, it will without doubt mean that certain practices are needed to sustain a distinctive identity, lest the Christian and the church inadvertently become as secular as the society in which they are located.

CONCLUSION

We are in a new reality—"the times they are a-changin'" and have been for a while. We need wisdom to guide the church's response, and in particular to guide those who are giving leadership to the church in an increasingly secular context. I would suggest that there are at least four potential sources for this wisdom, and I will be exploring these in the next four chapters.

First, I will consider how the witness of the exilic and postexilic prophets of the Old Testament has continuing and particularly relevant wisdom to offer. While not an exact parallel to our situation, there is plenty that is pertinent—enough that I would suggest that the Old Testament prophets, and particularly those who spoke to the people of Judah in exile, need to have pride of place in a program of theological education.

Second, it is also helpful to consider wisdom from the early church. Under secularity, the church is no longer privileged. We live in a post-Christendom world, and thus we might find wisdom from the *pre-Christendom* church—from before Christianity became the official religion of the land, when the Christian community was a minority presence. In particular, I am going to focus on Ambrose of Milan and Augustine of Hippo—looking to the wisdom of the fourth and early fifth centuries. Here too, I wonder if the early church should be privileged in a program of theological formation. When I was in seminary in the 1970s, my church history studies focused on the Protestant Reformation of the sixteenth century and the evangelical renewal movements of the late eighteenth century. All good, of course, but I wonder now if the main focus in a theological program, when it comes to the history of the church, should be on the wisdom and experience of the early church fathers and mothers.

Then third, it is good to consider the voices that emerge from historic minority churches. The church has always been a minority presence somewhere—Japan, India, China, the Middle East. What wisdom emerges from the experience of the church when it has always, for centuries, been a minority presence?

And fourth, there is much wisdom to be found in voices from Central and Western Europe—those who are further along the path of secularism. Here, my primary sources will be Dietrich Bonhoeffer, Jacques Ellul, and Lesslie Newbigin.

Are there other sources of wisdom? Certainly. We must lean into the powerful witness of theologians and spiritual writers from Gregory the Great to Bernard of Clairvaux to voices from both the Protestant and Catholic Reformations. Further, Bruce Hindmarsh and others have demonstrated the continuing relevance of the early evangelical movement.[10] Then also, we need to be on a journey of shared learning with voices from the postcolonial church of Africa and the Middle East. In my own country, we are learning what it means to be attentive to the wisdom of the new immigrant communities as well as indigenous peoples. We can be and must be learning together how to navigate these waters as we seek to be what we are called to be in this time and in this place.

While acknowledging these other sources, I have chosen to highlight voices that, it seems to me, have particular immediacy to the church in a post-Christian secular context precisely because they speak to what it means to be a religious minority presence. There is no doubt that the selection of these four is debatable. None of these provides us with the last word on what it means to be the church today, and many perspectives and insights can and must be added to these sources.

The next four chapters, then, will consider these four sources of wisdom. In chapter 7, having considered these four sources, I will return to the four responses outlined in this chapter and consider each of them, asking how the sources of wisdom might inform both the strengths and limitations of each of these responses.

---

[10]See D. Bruce Hindmarsh, *The Spirit of Early Evangelicalism: True Religion in a Modern World* (Oxford: Oxford University Press, 2018).

3

WISDOM FROM BABYLON

ATTENDING TO THE EXILIC
AND POSTEXILIC PROPHETS

HOW CAN THE EXPERIENCE OF JUDAH during the exile and after the exile, the experience of Diaspora Israel, contribute wisdom to the church in the twenty-first century—a church in a post-Christian secular society? Before speaking of what we can learn, I should point out that I am not claiming that there is a direct parallel between the experience of the people of Judah in exile and the contemporary experience of increased secularity. There are two—at least two—noteworthy contrasts or differences. First, and most notably, their exile was traumatic: Jerusalem was destroyed, families were horrifically disrupted, and the social infrastructure left in tatters. The contrast between that and our situation needs to be stressed when we hear church leaders bemoan the situation of the church in a post-Christian Western context. It is imperative that we not overstate our experience of exile as though we are suffering in a similar manner. And second, they moved—they underwent a forced migration from Judah to Babylon. They lived as a minority presence *in a foreign land.*

It was not a direct parallel, and yet the experience of exile and specifically the wisdom of the prophets who spoke into the exile provides the contemporary church in a secular society an opportunity to reconsider our contemporary situation. In particular, it prompts us to ask what it means to be a minority presence, and what aspects of the exilic experience might inform the life and mission of the church in our day.

THE EXILE AND THE POSTEXILIC EXPERIENCE

Jerusalem surrendered to the Babylonians in 597 BC. King Nebuchadnezzar took the king of Judah, Jehoiachin, off to Babylon and put his own regent in place back in Jerusalem. But when rebellion in Jerusalem threatened Babylonian control, the result was the full exile beginning in 586 BC. In the process, the city of Jerusalem was destroyed and the people of Judah experienced extraordinary suffering. The book of Lamentations is an extended poem that captures the sentiments of those who felt the full force of the destruction of Jerusalem. The underlying theme of the book is that God was not there in the face of a powerful enemy; they were deserted (Lamentations 1:1). They were forced to leave the land of their ancestors and live in the region of their archenemy.

Not all went into exile, however. There is evidence that a segment of the population, perhaps even a large segment, remained in the region of the former capital. This seems to have been the experience of the prophet Jeremiah, for example (see Jeremiah 40–43). And yet a sizable portion of the population did go into exile. This situation lasted until 539 BC when the Babylonians were defeated by the Persian empire of Cyrus. As described in Ezra and Nehemiah, Cyrus allowed for the return of the people to Judah. Further, Cyrus specifically decreed that the temple was to be rebuilt in Jerusalem (2 Chronicles 36:23-24). As Iain Provan and his colleagues note, this was not because Cyrus had a special interest in the religion of the people of Judah. Rather, this was typical of the foreign policy of Persia, which allowed certain people to sustain their religious identity.[1] Yet for the people of Judah this was an affirmation that the exile was over, and the theme of the rebuilding of the temple is central to the words of the prophets Haggai and Zechariah.

Even after the exile, though, the people of Judah were still a minority religious presence within the Persian Empire. The Persian defeat of the Babylonians did *not* mean the end of the exile. Ezra would speak of being "slaves in the land that you gave to our ancestors" under the Persians (Nehemiah 9:36-37). The seventy years of exile prophesied in Jeremiah

---

[1]Iain Provan, V. Philips Long, and Tremper Longman III, *A Biblical History of Israel*, rev. ed. (Louisville, KY: Westminster John Knox, 2015), 391. For those who want to read further on the exile, see in particular chapter 11.

29:10 seemed to extend for quite a long time—well into the Persian period and the Hellenistic period that followed.

And yet the consistent testimony of the prophets is that this is all part of the providential purposes of God, working through the ruling authorities—first the Babylonians and then the Persians. We see asides that witness that this situation was seen as providential: Jeremiah 29 speaks of seeking the welfare of the city "where I have sent you" (Jeremiah 29:7), and Ezra 7:27 observes that God "put . . . into the heart of the king to glorify the house of the LORD in Jerusalem." This surely needs to inform the way in which the church in a post-Christian secular society considers its situation and its response. It would make a substantive difference if we actually considered the possibility that our situation is providential.

While the books of Ezra and Nehemiah (notably Ezra 7–Nehemiah 13) tell the story of those who returned to Jerusalem after the edict of Cyrus, the book of Esther provides us with an account of those who did not return. They stayed in a foreign land; they were the first of the Diaspora that continues today in the Middle East, Europe, and North America. Esther was located within the royal court, and Mordecai, a civic official within the Persian government, seemed to have assimilated in the land of their captivity, adopting elements of the culture and social institutions of Persia.

What can we take from the witness of the prophets as they spoke into this experience of the people of Judah? The operative and recurring theme is surely that the genius of such an existence—thriving in the time of exile and Diaspora—is one of presence with a distinctive identity. The people are encouraged to be present and engaged, but to be and remain "other"—that is, to sustain an identity as the people of God. As Daniel Smith-Christopher notes, "The exile was both catastrophic and transformative for Hebrew existence (and thus for biblical theology)."[2] Yes, it was a tragedy, as is palpably evident in a reading of the book of Lamentations. But it also opened a new vision of what it means to be the people of God. Smith-Christopher suggests that we can speak of an exilic as well as a diasporic theology. He observes, building on the work of John

---

[2]Daniel Smith-Christopher, *A Biblical Theology of Exile* (Minneapolis: Fortress: 2002), 32.

Howard Yoder, Walter Brueggemann, and Stanley Hauerwas, that the heart of the matter for the people of God is to sustain a distinctive identity and culture while also cultivating a dynamic resistance. But—and this is the crucial piece—it is not the resistance of the "sword." Rather, Smith-Christopher—referencing Ezra and Nehemiah—notes a recurring theme in the attitude toward the Persian authorities: it is not one of warmth or gratitude, but definitely *deference*. Yet this deference always included the assumption that there was (and is) a higher authority—the authority of God alone.[3]

What is impressive about Esther and then also Daniel is precisely their capacity to sustain this tension—this dual identity. Lee Beach observes: "[Esther] is a model of perpetual cultural engagement: embedded in the culture, employing cultural norms, functioning as a full member of her society, but with a humility and sense of proportion that makes her distinct from those around her."[4] In her commentary on Esther, Carol Bechtel observes that the book is an extended meditation on how to live as a minority presence, and thus how the people of God can flourish with limited power. She uses the image of canoeing from the front of the boat—it is challenging, but it can be done.[5] Smith-Christopher notes of Esther, Daniel, Mordecai, and others: "All of them . . . face questions of remaining true to their identity in difficult times. Compromise is a constant temptation, assimilation a constant threat, but justice and exemplary behavior are the consistent advice of these works."[6] He goes on to observe that to be a minority presence—with limited power and influence—is not a bad or catastrophic thing in itself.

The experience of exile can give us a way to rethink and reimagine what it means to be the people of God. Nothing is gained by either being at war with our circumstances or overwrought by our situation. It is quite possible to be "in but not of" the social context and culture. The exile of Judah could be viewed as a time of decline and a regrettable development, or it might actually be a foretaste of what it truly means to be the church.

---

[3]Smith-Christopher, *A Biblical Theology of Exile*, 45.
[4]Lee Beach, *The Church in Exile: Living in Hope After Christendom* (Downers Grove, IL: IVP Academic, 2015), 77.
[5]Carol M. Bechtel, *Esther* (Louisville, KY: Westminster John Knox, 2002), 11.
[6]Smith-Christopher, *A Biblical Theology of Exile*, 190.

From this perspective, it is not so much a problem as an *opportunity* for a new way of thinking about the mission and the faith of the church.

Crucial in all of this is how we think about power. Resistance does not entail the exercise or leveraging of power per se for the very simple reason that, as the people of God in exile, they did not have power. Indeed, it would seem that the message is actually to reject the way of military or economic power and accept the limits of our political power. This does not mean that we do not develop political savvy. To the contrary, we need precisely to learn how to be truly political in our speech and advocacy. We do need to develop the political skill required to navigate this world, and this necessarily means knowing what it is to pursue principled compromise and what it means to speak truth to those who wield the levers of political, economic, and military power.

THE MESSAGE OF THE EXILIC PROPHETS

What are the key lessons from this source of wisdom for the church in a post-Christian and secular age? There are at least three areas that merit our attention:

- The need to remember the glory of God who judges humanity and demonstrates mercy

- The importance of sustaining a distinctive identity as the people of God

- The need to speak hope against the backdrop of lament

The glory of God: holiness and mercy. Nothing is so foundational to the witness of the prophets as the glory of God who stands holy and unassailable before the forces of darkness. Part of what impresses us in reading the prophets is that they do not despair in the face of the exile and the destruction of Jerusalem. Rather, they continue to both see and witness to the glory of God.

A keen example of this is the opening of the book of Ezekiel, where the prophet is among the exiles along the Chebar River and he sees a vision of God in the heavens (Ezekiel 1:1-3). What is noteworthy is that this vision is not happening in Jerusalem, in the temple. Instead, the prophet is among the exiles—far from Jerusalem. The people of Judah are perplexed that God has abandoned them and allowed the destruction of their homes and their city. But the witness of the prophet is that they are not alone; God is with them. The glory of God is revealed to them specifically in the exile.

This glory is revealed at all times in the beauty and majesty of the created order. But in the prophets in particular, there is a twofold manifestation of the glory of God that is deeply sobering and at the same time profoundly hopeful. First, the glory of God is revealed as the holy one of Israel; this contrasts dramatically with the sinfulness of humanity in general and the people of Judah in particular. He even calls them worse than Sodom at one point, which is about as low as it gets (Ezekiel 16:46-48). The point of Ezekiel and the other prophets is that judgment begins with the people of God.

Second, the prophets witness to the all-encompassing *mercy* of God. When the people of Judah acknowledge their sin, they find mercy in abundance. But the key is that we only know mercy when we name the reality of sin. Confession and repentance are integral to the capacity of the people of God to witness the glory of God. They can know with confidence that God will be their God and will restore their fortunes.

The call to sustain a distinctive identity. The exilic prophets have a second recurring emphasis for the people of Judah: they can and must remain the people of God when it comes to their ultimate allegiance. Yes, the people of God are residents in another land, but their loyalty belongs elsewhere. If this is lost, all is lost. This identity as the people of God is evident in a number of ways, but the most notable are in their worship and in their ethics or behavior.

First, they will worship the Lord God and him alone. Their affection, loyalty, and primary orientation will be toward the creator and redeemer of all things and the one to whom they owe their very existence. Despite their disappointment and perplexity at the fact that God seemingly had abandoned them—was not there when they faced their enemy—the insistence of the prophets is that God is still God, and God is still *their* God.

Second, God's people are a holy people who, as a fundamental mark of their lives in the world, live with a deep and palpable commitment to justice. Without doubt the witness of the prophets assumes that the people of God care about personal morality, yet what must not be missed is that personal holiness must necessarily be complemented by a commitment to social and economic holiness.

The religious tradition in which I was raised as a rule spoke of holiness as a question of personal sanctity in the quality and character of one's business dealings, morality, and dispositions. But the witness of the prophets suggests that there is a profound continuity between the personal and the social vision of what it means to be a holy person. The prophets insist that those who claim their identity in God would necessarily exhibit this in a commitment to social and economic justice. The two cannot be divorced.

Isaiah 58 is part of that section of Isaiah that moves beyond the immediate reference to the exile itself; the prophet is now anticipating the deliverance that is yet to come. His words are striking:

> Is not this the fast that I choose:
> > to loose the bonds of injustice,
> to undo the thongs of the yoke,
> > to let the oppressed go free,
> > and to break every yoke?
> Is it not to share your bread with the hungry,
> > and bring the homeless poor into your house;
> when you see the naked, to cover them,
> > and not to hide yourself from your own kin?
> Then your light shall break forth like the dawn,
> > and your healing shall spring up quickly;
> your vindicator shall go before you,
> > the glory of the LORD shall be your rear guard. (Isaiah 58:6-8)

These words assume that the people of Judah are a worshipping people; the point is that worship without a commitment to social justice is a sham. The two must go together—the integrity of our worship is evident in the quality of our relationships with those who are at the margins of society.

This has significant implications for what it means to be the church in a secular age, especially when we ask what comes to mind for the society around us when they consider the church. In a secular and pluralistic context, it may well be that what most marks the church is not a matter of personal morality, including sexual ethics—however important this is and however much sexual holiness must mark the church. Rather, what makes the church distinctive is the commitment to social holiness—an advocacy for the homeless, the immigrant, and the refugee, for those who have been victims of sexual assault, the vulnerable, and all who are subject to social, racial, and economic injustice.

Speaking hope against the backdrop of lament. Surely one of the great marks of the prophets was their capacity to speak hope in the face of very dark circumstances. If the church in a secular age is going to have leadership that can speak hope in like manner, we must recognize that the genius of the prophets was that they preached hope out of lament. Few have testified to this more powerfully than Walter Brueggemann, who insists that we need to speak to the experience of suffering. He writes in *The Prophetic Imagination*, "It is the task of prophetic ministry and imagination to bring people to engage their experiences of suffering to death."[7]

Then again, "In the hospital room we want it to be cheery, and in a broken marriage we want to imagine it will be all right. We bring the lewd promise of immortality everywhere, which is not a promise but only a denial of what history brings and what we are indeed experiencing."[8] In so doing there is no question that God is still God. And yet, as Brueggemann observes, the prophets give language to "the fear and the pain that individual persons want so desperately to share and to own but are not permitted to do so."[9] The prophets' words, their speaking, is neither "abrasive rejections" nor "maudlin assurances."[10] In this way the prophets give their hearers a "language of grief."[11]

For Brueggemann, the supreme example of this capacity to speak hope against the backdrop of lament is Jeremiah, of whom he writes:

---

[7]Walter Brueggemann, *The Prophetic Imagination* (Minneapolis: Fortress, 1978), 46.
[8]Brueggemann, *Prophetic Imagination*, 49.
[9]Brueggemann, *Prophetic Imagination*, 50.
[10]Brueggemann, *Prophetic Imagination*, 50.
[11]Brueggemann, *Prophetic Imagination*, 51.

The prophet is engaged in a battle for language, in an effort to create a different epistemology . . . the prophet is not addressing behavioral problems . . . he is not even pressing for repentance. . . . He has only the hope that the *ache* of God could penetrate the *numbness* of history.[12]

It is only then that a new movement of God can emerge. Only if we truly speak lament can we speak of hope. Brueggemann again: "Those who do not mourn will not be comforted and those who do not face the endings will not receive the beginnings . . . only grievers can experience their experiences and move on."[13]

I write this with the abiding impression from a funeral that I attended a while back. The one who had died in an accident was remembered as a father, grandfather, and friend with a kind of frivolity; there were no tears, no acknowledgment of the huge loss. The presiding minister insisted at the beginning that it was "okay to laugh," and thus began a series of reflections that were all about remembered jokes or quirks of personality or the joy of his companionship. But no tears, and little sense of the terrible loss that was now being papered over. Those present that day needed to be told it was okay to cry, to weep, and even to wail. The grandchildren needed to know that their tears were appropriate. The irony, of course, is that this is supremely a secular response to death: we deny the tragedy and "celebrate" life because we cannot face the pain.

The prophets remind us that lament is important, and that naming the reality of darkness and death is speaking to what is actually happening or has happened. Then, against the backdrop of lament, the prophets speak hope—hope when their hearers are prone to despair. The church in a secular age urgently needs to learn from the exilic prophets what it means to be a master of encouragement—speaking hope in the midst of anguish. Without this backdrop, any attempt to speak hope, to encourage, is instead a false comfort.

What does it mean to speak genuine hope and provide encouragement? Brueggemann speaks of two things. The first is memory; there is no hope without remembrance. We testify to history—to the story of God and the

---

[12]Brueggemann, *Prophetic Imagination*, 59 (Brueggemann's emphasis).
[13]Brueggemann, *Prophetic Imagination*, 60.

faithfulness of God. The second is language, "to recognize how singularly words, speech, language, and phrase shape consciousness and define reality."[14] By this is meant, at the very least, that we refuse to speak platitudes and, further, that we learn the art of timing—what Proverbs 15:23 speaks of as "a word in season." This is a learned art in part because, as Brueggemann notes, "prophetic hope easily lends itself to distortion. It can be made so grandiose that it does not touch reality; it can be trivialized so that it does not impact reality; it can be 'bread and circuses' so that it only supports and abets the general despair."[15] Thus, when it is done poorly, it merely makes things worse. When it is done well, it returns the community to a dynamic awareness of the faithfulness of God.

The genius of the prophets in speaking hope is twofold: (1) they did not overstate the predicament; and (2) they did not bring false hope. We read in Jeremiah 28 of a prophet named Hananiah; he was the purveyor of a false hope. He was saying that in two years the Lord would bring down Nebuchadnezzar and end the Babylonian exile and Jehoiachin would be restored to the throne. This was a false message of a longing that was not from God.

All of this assumes, of course, not only that we name our own experience of pain, suffering, and disappointment but also that we are not oblivious to the pain that is around us—in our neighborhoods, cities, countries, and our world. We gather on Sunday as a people who are deeply aware of the ways in which we live and work in a deeply fragmented world. Our worship is not a denial of or an escape from this world but rather a liturgical encounter with God wherein we can affirm that even in the darkness there is light. We will not despair but will lament for our world and speak hope to our world—not the hope of false sentimentality or religious cliché but the hope that is grounded in the history of God.

READING 1 PETER AS WISDOM FROM BABYLON

For wisdom from the Babylonian exile and the postexilic experience, we read Ezekiel, Jeremiah, and Lamentations, along with the texts from the

---

[14]Brueggemann, *Prophetic Imagination*, 66.
[15]Brueggemann, *Prophetic Imagination*, 68.

prophets who spoke and wrote from the Diaspora: Esther and Daniel. But another significant source for thinking about what it means to be in exile is 1 Peter, which takes many of the themes of exile and diaspora from the Hebrew prophets and incorporates them into the experience of the first-century church. Part of what makes 1 Peter a distinctive letter is that it is clearly written to a church in a diasporic or minority social position. The letter opens with: "To the exiles of the dispersion in Pontus, Galatia, Cappadocia, Asia, and Bithynia." The audience is mainly Gentile believers, and yet the author uses the language of diaspora in speaking of his readers as "aliens and exiles" (1 Peter 2:11).

The letter speaks of Rome as Babylon; thus 1 Peter is "wisdom from Babylon." Paul Achtemeier notes that this reference is a way of signaling that both the author and the readers are learning what it means to live in exile.[16] Thus we come to see that being a minority presence as the church is not an anomaly; it is the norm and will be increasingly so. As Douglas Harink notes, Peter does not use the language of exile as a *metaphor* for their situation. It is not that they are to live "as though they were in exile." Rather, they *are* in exile; they *are* an alien people (1 Peter 1:17). And consequently, he urges them to "live in reverent fear in your time of exile."[17] This letter thus complements and supplements the wisdom of the Old Testament exilic prophets in speaking to how the church is called to live as a minority religious presence in a pagan or pluralist world. This is the heart of the message— notably in 1 Peter 2:11–4:11.

Peter calls for a faithful engagement with society, specifically from a minority position. The apostle does not advocate for withdrawal from the world (a monastic seclusion). He does not advocate for abandoning society. Rather, he urges his readers to be present to their social context and setting—fully engaged. He further stresses that they are not to succumb to the values or mores of the world; they are aliens in this world and in their culture. They are, in other words, to be "in but not of." They

---

[16]Paul J. Achtemeier, *1 Peter: A Commentary on 1 Peter*, Hermeneia (Minneapolis: Fortress, 1996), 354.

[17]Douglas Harink, *1 & 2 Peter*, Brazos Theological Commentary on the Bible (Grand Rapids, MI: Brazos Press, 2009). See his excellent reflection on the theme of exile and the implications for reading 1 Peter on pages 28-38.

are to be fully present but not aligned with the values of the society in which they are located.

Peter often stresses the theme of not being "of" the culture or the society. He writes, for example, "Like obedient children, do not be conformed to the desires that you formerly had in ignorance" (1 Peter 1:14); and further, "abstain from the desires of the flesh" (1 Peter 1:11). They are to be a holy people—set apart in their identity and marked by a particular pattern of behavior.

When it comes to being fully present to the society, he stresses two things. On the one hand, he notes that his readers are to be marked by a commitment to good works. They are to live and be in the society as a people marked by a commitment to the civic good. And then, further, this engagement is to be marked by a depth and grace of character; he even suggests that they might "win over" their neighbors with their behavior as much as their words (1 Peter 2:11-12).

Further, Peter urges them to live graciously within the systems of human authority in which they have been placed (1 Peter 2:13–3:7). This is a significant theme in the letter; he urges his readers to "for the Lord's sake accept the authority of every human institution" (1 Peter 2:13), and goes on to speak of civic authority (governors), then of slaves/masters, and then also of family systems. Christians, in other words, are to be law-abiding citizens who know how to live and work within authoritative communities and structures—though it is important to note that 1 Peter 2:17 suggests that civil obedience is not absolute; we honor civil authorities but we fear God.

Peter recognizes that this will not be easy. If Christians sustain their distinctive identity, even if they are law-abiding and civic-minded citizens, they will experience grief. Peter has no patience if they suffer for doing wrong, but he makes it clear that Christians in a minority position could well suffer for their faith—precisely because they are committed to the good. He urges them to not be blindsided by this: "Do not be surprised at the fiery ordeal that is taking place among you to test you" (1 Peter 4:12). He says to rejoice rather than be humiliated, for in suffering they are in alignment with Christ, who in like manner suffered.

In response to suffering, Christians are to continue to do good (1 Peter 4:19); they are to be patient and gracious in the midst of suffering (1 Peter 2:23); and they are to be ready to respond to those who ask about their faith: "Always be ready to make a defense to who anyone who demands . . . an accounting for the hope that is within you" (1 Peter 3:15). But as they speak and make an account of their faith, they are to "do it with gentleness and reverence" (1 Peter 3:16a). There is no place for the harsh word.

To summarize, 1 Peter clearly assumes that it is possible to flourish as a minority presence and to be an authentic witness to the reign of Christ. Indeed, Harink suggests that 1 Peter actually calls the church to see its unique opportunity.[18] That is, 1 Peter teaches us not to bemoan our situation but to leverage its transformative potential. Presence within the society may well be marked by grief and difficulty but this does not diminish the potential of redemptive engagement. And further, what it looks like to be an agent of grace is not responding with anger or a harsh word, but with "gentleness and reverence."

CONCLUSION

As we think about how the exilic and postexilic prophets can inform our present situation, we might do well to consider again what is likely the most quoted passage from the prophet Jeremiah:

> These are the words of the letter that the prophet Jeremiah sent from Jerusalem to the remaining elders among the exiles, and to the priests, the prophets, and all the people, whom Nebuchadnezzar had taken into exile from Jerusalem to Babylon. This was after King Jeconiah, and the queen mother, the court officials, the leaders of Judah and Jerusalem, the artisans, and the smiths had departed from Jerusalem. The letter was sent by the hand of Elasah son of Shaphan and Gemariah son of Hilkiah, whom King Zedekiah of Judah sent to Babylon to King Nebuchadnezzar of Babylon. It said: Thus says the LORD of hosts, the God of Israel, to all the exiles whom I have sent into exile from Jerusalem to Babylon: Build houses and live in them; plant gardens and eat what they produce. Take wives and

---

[18]Harink, *1 & 2 Peter*, 36.

have sons and daughters; take wives for your sons, and give your daughters in marriage, that they may bear sons and daughters; multiply there, and do not decrease. But seek the welfare of the city where I have sent you into exile, and pray to the LORD on its behalf, for in its welfare you will find your welfare. (Jeremiah 29:1-7)

In light of the previous discussion, two things emerge from these words. The first is that the prophet twice emphasizes that it is God that has sent them into exile—in verse 4 and then again in verse 7 with "seek the welfare of the city to where I have sent you." These asides should suggest to contemporary readers who sense they are now "in exile" that perhaps this is something they can view providentially. And second, it was this awareness that their exile was not an accident that freed them to be full residents of the city—building houses, planting gardens, and seeking the peace and welfare of the society in which they had been placed. As Harink stresses, and as noted above, the position of exile is perhaps inherent in what it means to be the people of God. It is not an aberration but fundamental to what it means to be the church.

Could it be, then, that the current social, cultural, political, and religious location of the church in the West is actually providential? If so, it means that rather than wringing our hands and despairing for the church and for our culture, we must instead ask what it might mean if this is "of God"—if this situation is providential. Starting from this posture dramatically reshapes how the church responds; we would seek more to ask what opportunities we have for transformation.

We need to keep in our minds the words of the prophet Isaiah who, in speaking to the people anticipating exile, wrote:

But now thus says the LORD,
    he who created you, O Jacob,
    he who formed you, O Israel:
Do not fear, for I have redeemed you;
    I have called you by name, you are mine.
When you pass through the waters, I will be with you;
    and through the rivers, they shall not overwhelm you;

when you walk through fire you shall not be burned,
  and the flame shall not consume you.
For I am the Lord your God,
  the Holy One of Israel, your Savior.
I give Egypt as your ransom,
  Ethiopia and Seba in exchange for you.
Because you are precious in my sight,
  and honored, and I love you,
I give people in return for you,
  nations in exchange for your life.
Do not fear, for I am with you. (Isaiah 43:1-5)

Why is it that they will go through the fire and through the floods but will not be burned, and they will not be overcome? Because they belong to God, and God will go with them. Therefore, "do not fear" (verse 1), and then again, "Do not fear, for I am with you" (verse 5). Similarly, 1 Peter concludes with a call that seems to link "the adversary" to the church's potential vulnerability to being afraid and anxious; thus he calls his readers to humility and to "cast all your anxiety on him, because he cares for you" (1 Peter 5:7).

As I will stress again and again when speaking of what it means to be the church and to provide leadership for the church in a secular age, the greatest threat to the church is not external but internal. The greatest threat is fear, not the society or culture in which we are located. Thus, it is simply imperative that we learn to address our fears and live with confidence and grace in the providential care of God.

4

PERSPECTIVE AND WISDOM
FROM THE EARLY CHURCH

BY "THE EARLY CHURCH" we mean that period from the death of the original apostles through the sixth century, including Origen of Alexandria, John Chrysostom, Gregory of Nyssa, Irenaeus, Tertullian, Gregory the Great, and those that will be the focus of this chapter: Ambrose of Milan and Augustine of Hippo. For much of this period, Christianity was a minority faith in a pluralist and pagan environment. But the major shift happened in the fourth century with the conversion of the Roman Emperor Constantine in AD 312 and then the Edict of Milan in 313, when it was declared that Christianity would be tolerated along with other religions—that is, that Christianity would now be legal.

The next noteworthy transition came in AD 380, when Emperor Theodosius declared that Christianity would be the official religion of the empire. This began what historians typically call "Christendom": not merely Christianity, which was founded by the apostles, but now there is the phenomenon of the state church, wherein citizenship and religious affiliation are one and the same. One's baptismal certificate is proof of national identity.

This union of state and church survived the Reformation despite the insistence of the Anabaptists that this violates Christian identity. If you lived in Sweden or Denmark you were Lutheran; if you lived in Spain or Ireland or Croatia you were Catholic. If you were Russian or Romanian or Serbian or Bulgarian, you were Orthodox. The church in England for many Christians was the Church of England until the Baptists duly protested and faced the consequences—not always happy ones. The British monarch was and still is the head of the Church of England, and the

British Prime Minister appoints the Archbishop of Canterbury. In reaction to Christendom, the United States was formed on the assumption that church and state would be utterly separated—as a matter of constitutional conviction with a commitment to freedom of religion. (Yet, as we have seen, many in the United States assume that it too is a Christian country and that this is part of its birthright.)

We must, then, make a distinction between Christendom and Christianity and recognize that Christianity can flourish even with the demise of Christendom. Indeed, many would argue that it can *only* flourish if there is a true separation of church and state.

One of the sources of learning for the church in a post-Christendom social context is surely the experience of the pre-Christendom church. As with each source of learning for the church in a secular context, the parallels are not one-to-one, yet there is much wisdom here. And of course, Ambrose and Augustine do not represent the only perspective from the early church. But at the very least, they provide a powerful witness and wisdom that has and will have continuing relevance to the church in the West.

In looking for representatives of pre-Christendom Christian experience and witness, Augustine is an easy call. He is essential reading for the church in a post-Christian secular society. Ambrose is an important resource for a variety of reasons, including his link with Augustine's experience of coming into Christian faith and his articulation of what it means to sustain a trinitarian faith. But it is also notable that he gives us an example of someone trying to navigate a complex political and cultural situation. That is where we begin.

AMBROSE, AUGUSTINE, AND THE CULTIVATION OF POLITICAL INFLUENCE

Ambrose was born in Augusta Treverorum (modern-day Trier, Germany) in AD 339. He was broadly educated and moved into civil service in his thirties. When the bishop of Milan died, there was tension about who would succeed him in that Milan was deeply divided between those who followed Nicene Christianity (the Council of Nicaea had been in AD 325) and those who were Arian in their religious affiliation. Ambrose had a positive reputation from his work in the civil service and was viewed as one who would be acceptable to both parties. He was therefore elected, even though he was not yet baptized; strangely enough, he was baptized, ordained a priest, and elected bishop on the same day.

As bishop, Ambrose gives us an example of a religious leader who engaged civic authorities and insisted on the independence of the church. One case involved the Empress Justina, an Arian, who became empress ten years after Ambrose became bishop. She felt that one of the churches in Milan should be reserved for Arian worship. But as bishop, Ambrose insisted that this fell under his authority and he rebuffed her despite the fact that she had military support that he could never match.

Another example of his insistence that the church and its leaders were independent of government authority came when he exercised church discipline on Emperor Theodosius after the horrific slaughter of thousands of people in Thessalonica in 390. Theodosius had originally authorized the massacre as an act of revenge for the killing of a Roman official, but then changed his mind too late and it went ahead. In response, Ambrose forced Theodosius into an extended time of penance.

In both cases, Ambrose insisted that the church is an independent entity, not beholden to the state—indeed, that the church is the *conscience* of the state. Ambrose would not be beholden to the emperor, and he persisted in calling the state to account for behavior that clearly was a violation of justice. In other words, Ambrose sustained his independence from civilian authorities.

Augustine was born in Thagaste, northern Africa, in AD 354 and died in 430. He is in many respects the premier voice and theologian of Western Christianity through the sixteenth century. Below I will rehearse his journey to faith and the impact of Ambrose on his life. But first, consider how he spoke to the matter of church and state, most notably in his magisterial *The City of God*.

The immediate context for this work is the decline of Rome. Rome was conquered and pillaged in 410 by Alaric and the Visigoths. Those fleeing to northern Africa suggested that the reason Rome fell was because it had become Christian; the people had not been faithful to the ancestral deities. Augustine's rebuttal provides his read on all that Rome represented: culture, human accomplishment, intellectual tradition, but also how the city was marked by violence and bloodshed and the abuse of power fueled by the sin of pride.

Others viewed Rome as an emerging Christian empire. Augustine likewise criticized this opinion; for him the work of God was more subtle, and this included his conviction that God worked through a suffering church. Thus Augustine would insist that no one knows for sure the purposes of God or where God is at work and in what ways. In other words, Augustine resisted two opposite impulses: to demonize society and culture or to naively equate human society in any form with the kingdom of God.

The primary theme of *The City of God*, written in installments between 413 and 426, is the interplay between the sphere of God's rule (the city of God) and the sphere of human culture and accomplishment (the city of man). In both cities, the agenda is the pursuit of happiness—within the confines of mortal existence, but then also within eternity, which for Augustine is a perpetual sabbath. Using the trope of the two cities, Augustine interprets his times in a way that is remarkably relevant for the church in the twenty-first century. Those who want to draw on Augustine as a source of wisdom for what it means to live and work in a post-Christian West should at the very least read book XIX. *The City of God* is like a series of essays where the author repeats himself and comes back to earlier points so that he can reinforce what he has written earlier, but book XIX captures the heart of the argument.[1]

Chapters 1–3 of book XIX provide the reader with a review of classical wisdom on the nature of the supreme good—notably from the Platonic tradition. Augustine concludes that our greatest happiness is found in the pursuit of virtue. Toward the end of chapter 3, he observes that the highest form of Christian experience is neither the contemplative life nor the active life but the "composite"—what will emerge in later writers, notably in the Jesuit tradition, as "the contemplative in action." The idea that we can be contemplatives in the active life is essential for what Augustine will say later about the call for a Christian presence in the city of man. I will come back to the importance of this in the final chapter.

---

[1]Augustine, *The City of God*, book XIX, www.newadvent.org/fathers/120119.htm.

Augustine goes on to insist that a happy life is marked by a communal dimension. He opens chapter 5 by observing that the life of a wise man must be social; the supreme good is found not in isolation but in community (this is the focus of chapters 5–17). Chapter 8, midway through an extended section on living at peace with our neighbors, is an extended reflection on friendship. Augustine acknowledges that when we have a friend we bear not only our own pain but their pain as well, yet his main theme is that friendship is a source of deep delight and consolation.

Key for our purposes here is Augustine's observation in this section that there is a great deal in common between the city of man and the city of God. Could this continuity between the two cities actually be the key to an authentic Christian witness in the earthly city? If this is the case, then wise Christian witness is not marked by an adversarial posture toward the culture in which we live. We can celebrate the good in our society, and we can work in common cause with non-Christians toward this good.

In chapters 18–20, Augustine lays out various opinions on happiness, then speaks specifically to a Christian vision, most notably in chapter 20. He examines the four cardinal virtues and demonstrates that each does not lead to ultimate happiness until and unless there is faith: Christian faith is essential to true happiness.

In chapters 21–27 we come to his political vision, with a theological digression in chapters 22–23. Augustine wrote *The City of God* in response to a church that lived with the constant temptation to flee the city and hunker down in a monastic community where one did not have to live with the pressure points and temptations of the "city of man." The most notable example of this was Benedict of Nursia, founder of Benedictine monasticism, who was born about fifty years after Augustine's death. While Benedict was noteworthy in this regard, the monastic impulse had been a powerful one in the church from as early as the second century. Augustine makes the case that though the Roman Empire is marked by earthly and transitory goods, there is a place and need for those who will serve the common good even if their primary and ultimate orientation is the city of God.[2] Augustine observes in chapter 26 that the two cities commingle, and that therefore we can seek the peace of the city (he references Jeremiah 29); we can pray for civic leaders and, as we are able, work with them for the common good.

If Ambrose provides us with an example of a church leader trying, in very complex and politically convoluted times, to be fully present to his social and political context while sustaining independence for the church and for the faith, Augustine provides the theological framework and vision for that stance. He is resolved to seek the common good with an affirmation that the "city of man" is not all evil and can know some measure of virtue, while all along insisting that ultimate virtue and happiness is only found where faith flourishes—in the city of God.

Thus, as James K. A. Smith suggests in *Awaiting the King*, the church can sustain what he calls a holy ambivalence in our relationship to the political—a healthy distance that affirms the legitimate place of the state and the civic square but where our ultimate hope is the reign of Christ that is yet to come (thus "awaiting" the King).[3] This means that we neither dismiss political engagement nor overstate what is possible; we discern and respond always in an ad hoc manner to opportunities as they present themselves—opportunities to collaborate toward penultimate ends.[4] We do not demonize or dismiss the public square; it is part of our world and our space. We must work toward a common good that as much as possible opens up space for communities of faith.[5]

What we need, of course, is a public theology—a theological vision for engaging the public square—that keeps the Christian community engaged but with a healthy dose of skepticism. By *skepticism* I do not mean cynicism. I mean rather a sober realization of the limits of what *can* happen—for, indeed, we only *witness* to the kingdom; we do not bring about the kingdom. We turn from both quietism and overzealous

---

[2]Augustine, *City of God*, book XIX, paragraph 17.

[3]James K. A. Smith, *Awaiting the King: Reforming Public Theology* (Grand Rapids, MI: Baker Academic, 2017), 16.

[4]Smith, *Awaiting the King*, 17.

[5]Smith, *Awaiting the King*, 219. Smith references Augustine, who in turn references 1 Timothy 2:2 ("that we may lead a quiet and peaceable life").

activities that assume somehow that we can bring about the kingdom.[6] We are pilgrims and exiles, *and* we are engaged with the earthly city. Even though our ultimate identity and citizenship is in the city of God, we participate in the common good, but not with illusions. We recognize that there are limits to what can happen this side of the kingdom that is yet to come.

Yes, Smith insists, we are political animals. But what makes the community of faith powerfully political is not the level of its engagement with the civic square as rather its capacity to cultivate a distinctive identity as the people of God, an identity that is formed by a very distinctive habit of liturgical practice.[7] And this leads naturally to this next point—the significance of the catechumenate.

AMBROSE, AUGUSTINE, AND THE EARLY CHRISTIAN CATECHUMENATE

A second notable contribution from Ambrose, Augustine, and the early church is the catechumenate. We urgently need to recover the vital place of catechesis—best defined simply as "religious instruction." This is not just any teaching but specifically teaching in the faith that fosters spiritual growth toward maturity in Christ. I am intentionally using this older word on the premise that we need to recover this ancient spiritual practice. My reflections here are a prologue to chapter 9, where I will stress in more detail that in a post-Christian, pluralist, and secular society churches need to be much more intentional regarding initiating Christians into the faith and becoming more vibrant teaching-learning communities.

There are many examples from the ancient church of diverse approaches to Christian initiation.[8] My focus here—in large measure because of its influence in Catholic circles in the late twentieth and twenty-first centuries—will be on the late fourth and early fifth century catechumenate of Ambrose and Augustine. To appreciate the significance of the catechumenate in the early church, we first need to be aware

---

[6]Smith, *Awaiting the King*, 224.

[7]Smith, *Awaiting the King*, 213.

[8]See chapter 1 of William Harmless, *Augustine and the Catechumenate*, rev. ed. (Collegeville, MN: Liturgical Press, 2014), for an overview of examples from the third and fourth centuries.

of how they understood religious experience, most notably the experience of conversion. For the ancients, and for Augustine in particular, conversion is not so much a punctiliar experience as a *journey*. Augustine's conversion to Christian faith is a series of events, none of which in itself constituted his conversion. Each of these events represents a notable step toward faith, though it should be said that these "steps" can as often as not only be appreciated in retrospect.

Augustine's story. Augustine's conversion narrative makes up the first part of his *Confessions*. There we learn that Augustine grew up in Thagaste, northern Africa, with a pagan father but a God-fearing Christian mother. Though his mother sought to raise him in the Christian faith, as a young man he was drawn to Manichaeism, and for upwards of nine years this was the intellectual and spiritual space in which he lived. He was attracted to Manichaeism because it gave him a way to make sense of the issue of evil and pain in the world. Evil, from this perspective, did not originate in God; it had a different and eternal source.

From Thagaste, on an intellectual quest, Augustine headed to Carthage and then to Rome, and along the way he was increasingly influenced by and taken with Neoplatonist perspectives. Eventually he arrived in Milan and came under the influence of the bishop of Milan, Ambrose.

There were other Christian influences on Augustine before this, such as Simplicianus, who urged him to be reading the Scriptures. But the most notable influence came from the bishop, particularly through his preaching. Ambrose's skills in rhetoric impressed Augustine so much that he chose to be present every Sunday to hear him preach.[9] At first he just wanted to hear great rhetoric, but in time he came to see that the faith being preached was truth, liberating truth, that he could not ignore. Slowly, he left behind his Manichaeism and became more open to the possibilities of faith and a personal call to faith in Christ. Soon after, he resolved to be a catechumen of the church.[10] He entered into a process overseen by Ambrose himself—a time of instruction and

---

[9]Augustine, *The Confessions of St. Augustine*, trans. John K. Ryan (London: Doubleday, 1960), VI.6.4.

[10]Augustine, *Confessions*, V.4.25.

training in Christianity with a focus on the creeds and the doctrines of the faith and an introduction into the moral vision of this faith. The catechumenate also included a time of exorcisms, with the intention being that one would move toward baptism with a body and soul freed of all impurities.

After an extended time, with much turmoil of soul, Augustine was in a retreat setting and in a garden heard the words *tolle, lege* ("pick up and read") spoken by a child. In tears he turned to the text before him, the words of Romans 13:13-14, and the effect was immediate.[11] At the Easter vigil in AD 387, he was baptized at the Milan Cathedral.

The catechumenate under Ambrose and Augustine. While the encounter in the garden was transformative, it can only be seen within the context of the catechumenate. The catechumenate assumes that there is an interior process, directed by the Spirit, by which a person comes to faith—thus Augustine's garden experience. And yet this interior experience does not happen in a vacuum; it is informed and mediated by the church. Augustine's conversion included but cannot be reduced to the garden experience because that experience could only have happened if and as Augustine was actually participating in the life of the church—and especially the catechumenate.

Christianity flourished in the pre-Constantine Greco-Roman pagan social and cultural environment before it became the religion of the empire. One of the reasons for this flourishing—not the only, but one reason—was the catechumenate. Some read the book of Acts and conclude that in the early church baptism followed immediately on a confession of faith. And perhaps it did. But by the fourth century, the time of Ambrose and Augustine, the church practiced an intentional delay in the rites of initiation, including baptism, during which those who expressed an interest in Christian faith were incorporated into committed Christian community.

Gerald Sittser makes the case that the catechumenate was needed because of the significant contrast between paganism and Christianity. A bridge needed to be built. Crossing this bridge, Sittser insists, was

---

[11] Augustine, *Confessions*, VIII.11.29.

rigorous. Christianity was attractive, but it was not easy to "get in."[12] An easy conversion was neither appropriate nor helpful; those making the transition into Christian faith were learning a whole new language with a radically different belief system and way of life that initially was completely alien to them.[13] Sittser quotes Rodney Stark, who speaks of how the early church was marked by "permeable boundaries": it was distinct from the society around it yet engaged with the pagan world. One of the ways it sustained this "distinct but engaged" dynamic was through the catechumenate.[14]

The church in the West in the twenty-first century faces a similar challenge in helping people coming to faith transition from a completely secular mindset and heart orientation to a genuinely Christian faith. Our situation is not in direct parallel to the world of Ambrose and Augustine, yet there is much wisdom for us represented in the ancient catechumenate.

AMBROSE, AUGUSTINE, AND TRINITARIAN INTERIORITY

In attending to perspectives that arise from the early church and in particular from Ambrose and Augustine, we also need to speak of the cultivation of *interiority*. Here it is helpful to begin with Augustine and then move back to the theological and liturgical vision and practices of Ambrose.

Augustine and the interior life. Louis Dupré is an astute observer of the contemporary secular context who observes that the only way to navigate this world is with an intentionally cultivated interiority. In an interview titled "Seeking Christian Interiority," Dupré responds to a question raised by Alasdair MacIntyre and others regarding whether we need to choose a way of life that is subject to religious practices along the lines of Benedict of Nursia—a kind of what is mentioned above as the "Benedict Option."[15] Dupré notes that spiritual or religious practice is

---

[12]Gerald Sittser, "The Catechumenate and the Rise of Christianity," *Journal of Spiritual Formation and Soul Care* 6.2 (Nov 2013): 183.

[13]Sittser, "The Catechumenate," 191.

[14]Sittser, "The Catechumenate," 182.

[15]"Seeking Christian Interiority: An Interview with Louis Dupré," *Christian Century*, July 16-23, 1997, 654-60.

appropriate, but only as we attend to the wisdom of Augustine, whom he describes as "the master of interior life."

Dupré observes that the Benedictine approach would only be an escape from the world, a flight from a broken civilization without the cultivation of interiority. He references Karl Rahner's observation that the Christianity of the future will be mystical or there will be no Christian faith at all. Cultivating faith from within is a "daunting task," but it is the only way that the church will be able to engage our culture with integrity and a coherent faith. In a deeply fragmented world, we need to resist the temptation to yield to what he calls "ultraconservative religious or political movements" motivated by nostalgia rather than an authentic engagement with the current times. These movements, unfortunately, are motivated more by seeking an ordered society rather than one that is truly informed by the truth of the gospel. Augustine learned to encounter God as not merely truth, morality, or order but as a personal and transformative presence. He demonstrated a deep awareness of and attentiveness to the inner movements of his heart that was marked by a remarkable honesty. In the *Confessions*, he makes clear that this was the secret of his whole life, work, and vision for the church.

When we speak about interiority as witnessed to by Augustine, several dimensions of human experience come to mind. First and most fundamentally, Augustine addressed interiority through the lens of spiritual autobiography; he used memory as a vehicle for making sense of his own personal and interior engagement with God. When we do this, we come to know God by attending to the ways in which we see the footprints of the Spirit in our inner experience.

Second, this interiority requires the willingness to *name* the reality of our interior lives. For Augustine, this meant facing the darkness of his heart with brutal honesty. We are not looking for nice and pleasant feelings; rather, we are seeking to know truly what is happening and to name it— even if it means that we come up against our disordered desires.

Third, this interiority always comes about through the goodness of God in whom we find our true home—our true rest. We are brutally honest in naming the darkness and the tortured experience that it inevitably creates, but this is worth the pain and discomfort because it opens up the possibility of an experience like what Augustine had in the garden.

It must be stressed that the interior life we seek is a very *Christian* interior life. Anyone attending to the wisdom of the ancient church needs to read books 1–9 of the *Confessions*, but it is books 10–13 that locate Augustine's experience in the context of the work of God in creation. We must hear the call of Augustine to a trinitarian interiority that is focused on the incarnate, crucified, and ascended Lord.

I will return in chapter 12 to the need for cultivating interiority, but the main point for now is this: "cultural Christians" will not be able to navigate the social, cultural, and religious dynamics of a secular age with any kind of intellectual and emotional resilience. We need to be, as in Rahner's remark referenced above, intentionally *mystical*: deeply connected with our own interior selves and thus deeply connected with God. We must learn to find our true home in God, and no one can do this for us. Each of us individually needs to cultivate this capacity. Further, this has to be an intentionally cultivated awareness and disposition within our faith communities.

Ambrose's trinitarian preaching and hymns. As mentioned above, we must cultivate interiority, but not just any interiority will do. In an age of the "spiritual but not religious," we must turn to Ambrose (and Augustine, but particularly Ambrose at this point) to learn how to cultivate a *trinitarian* interiority.

Augustine's inner experience of grace to which he testifies in the *Confessions* arose in the context of the liturgy and preaching at the cathedral in Milan under the leadership of Ambrose. In his sermons and writings, Ambrose was virtually obsessed with the doctrine of the Trinity. Of particular note is the prescient essay *On the Holy Spirit*, where he insisted again and again on the error of two of his opponents.[16] The first, the Arians, spoke of Jesus as distinct from the Father but not of the same essence of the Father—and thus not God like the Father and, by

---

[16]In *On the Holy Spirit*, III.16.117, Ambrose condemns both the Sabellians and the Arians. He also challenges the Apollinarians, who would separate the two natures of Christ (Christ is perfect man and perfect God).

implication, the Holy Spirit (who is at best a lesser being but not of the same essence as the Father). The second, the Sabellians, spoke of the full divinity of Son and Spirit but suggested that there is no Trinity per se. Rather, there is nothing but a sequence of divine expressions: one God who first appears as Father, then as Son, and supremely as Spirit.

Ambrose claimed that both got the nature of God deeply wrong, and that the only hope for an authentic Christian experience is to have one's inner life anchored in an orthodox understanding of the Holy Trinity. He insisted on the full divinity of the Son and Spirit—but more, the distinction between them. Father, Son, and Holy Spirit are each fully God, equal in authority, glory, and power, but also one and undivided, distinct but inseparable. It was this vision of God that anchored and infused his preaching and liturgical leadership. He pressed this point because he was convinced that our faith requires an appreciation of the Trinity; as he wrote, "the coherence of your soul is lessened if you do not believe the unity of the Godhead in the Trinity."[17] It is knowing, loving, and living in dynamic fellowship with the Trinity that gives coherence to our inner life—to our interior experience. It thus follows that when singing we affirm God as "Holy, Holy, Holy." In repeating this not twice but three times, "even in a hymn you may understand the distinction of Persons in the Trinity, and the oneness of the Godhead and while they say this they proclaim God."[18]

I will come back to Ambrose and hymns, but first it is important to emphasize the impact that this vision of the triune God had. Augustine's journey to faith happened within the context of the week-in, week-out preaching of Ambrose at the cathedral. Slowly but surely, the Scriptures, preached through the lens of the vision of a triune God, did their work in the heart of the hearers, including Augustine and the other catechumens. Augustine came to understand and feel the elegance of Scripture and its power. He speaks in the *Confessions* of how pride—intellectual arrogance—kept him at first from receiving the Word. He was impressed by

---

[17]Ambrose, *On the Holy Spirit*, III.3.14, in *St. Ambrose: Select Works and Letters*, ed. Philip Schaff and Henry Wace, trans. H. de Romestin, E. de Romestin, and H. T. F. Duckworth, A Select Library of the Nicene and Post-Nicene Fathers of the Christian Church, Second Series (New York: Christian Literature Company, 1896), 10:138.

[18]Ambrose, *On the Holy Spirit*, III.16.110.

Ambrose's rhetoric, but in the end it was the Scriptures themselves that needed to penetrate his heart. This encounter with the Scriptures took place in the context of Ambrose's clear trinitarian vision of God.

Finally, we should consider the impact of Ambrose's trinitarian liturgical leadership. Ambrose is credited with being the father of Western hymnody—the form of music that dominated Christian liturgy until the end of the twentieth century.[19] It is intriguing that Augustine refers to the hymns of the Milan cathedral in *Confessions*. As he thinks back over his experience and journey to faith, he observes that "the Church in Milan had not long before begun to worship with this form of consolation and exhortation, wherein with great fervor the brethren sing together in voice and heart."[20] He goes on to note that this practice of hymn singing was being taken up in congregations "throughout other parts of the world."[21]

Those familiar with Wesleyan-Methodism would appreciate the reference to fervor in singing—the equivalent to John Wesley's call to "sing lustily and with good courage" unto the Lord. And followers of Luther, for whom singing was praying twice—with head and heart—would appreciate the reference to "voice and heart." But here, what is striking regarding Augustine's observation is that the hymn singing served a dual purpose.

First, it was to comfort and encourage. Augustine here speaks of "consolation," then later in the same section of how "hymns and canticles should be sung, so that the people would not become weak through tedium and sorrow."[22]

Second, the singing of hymns was for "exhortation"; that is, it provided theological instruction. Ambrose did not just talk about the Trinity; he had the congregation sing the Trinity, and sing fervently. If they got it—if they were truly formed and informed and transformed by the trinitarian God—it was not merely a matter of understanding with the mind but actually entering into this extraordinary reality. Ambrose confronted heresy by having the congregation sing their trinitarian faith. To use an

---

[19]For more on Ambrose and hymnology, see Coleman Ford, "Ambrose of Milan and His Anti-Arian Hymns," Center for Ancient Christian Studies, www.ancientchristianstudies.com /blog/2015/4/8/ambrose-of-milan-and-his-anti-arian-hymns.

[20]Augustine, *Confessions*, trans. John K. Ryan (New York: Doubleday, 1960), IX.7.15.

[21]Augustine, *Confessions*, IX.7.15.

[22]Augustine, *Confessions*, IX.7.15.

ancient expression: *lex orandi lex credendi. Lex orandi,* how we pray, will shape what we believe, *lex credendi.* What we believe and hold to be true in our vision of life and work and relationships is shaped not merely by teaching and learning. Our understanding, the truth that penetrates heart and mind, is also formed by our worship, our shared prayers.

Here is an example of an Ambrose hymn—this one sung during Advent in celebration of the incarnation:

> Come, thou Redeemer of the earth,
> and manifest thy virgin-birth
> let every age adoring fall;
> such birth befits the God of all.
>
> Begotten of no human will,
> but of the Spirit, though art still
> the Word of God, in flesh arrayed,
> the Saviour, now to us displayed.
>
> From God the Father he proceeds,
> to God the Father back he speeds,
> runs out his course to death and hell,
> returns on God's high throne to dwell.
>
> O equal to thy Father, thou!
> Gird on thy fleshly mantle now,
> the weakness of our mortal state
> with deathless might invigorate.
>
> Thy cradle here shall glitter bright,
> and darkness glow with new-born light,
> no more shall night extinguish day,
> where love's bright beams their power display.
>
> O Jesu, virgin-born, to thee
> eternal praise and glory be,
> whom with the Father we adore
> and Holy Spirit, evermore. Amen.[23]

---

[23]Translated by J. M. Neal, https://hymnary.org/text/come_thou_redeemer_of_the_earth_and _man.

The hymn celebrates the Son who while equal with the Father now bears our flesh, who was begotten by the Spirit and now sits on God's throne, and who with the Father and the Spirit is adored. The point is that in singing the Trinity—not once, but again and again—we are formed by this vision of God and of our world.

This suggests that there is something problematic with contemporary songs and worship choruses that lack trinitarian depth and breadth. What or who we worship, we in turn believe; who we worship, if it is anything or anyone other than the triune God, is our own fabrication. The God of the Scriptures self-reveals as a triune God—Father, Son, and Spirit. Thus, only when we worship God as triune do we worship in truth, and only then are we formed in the truth. Only then do we have a true interiority.

Augustine picks up this emphasis on the Trinity. It is an important point of reference toward the end of the *Confessions,* and eventually he would publish his magisterial *The Trinity*—his magnus opus on the subject. But he comes to this appreciation and articulation of the meaning of the Trinity through a process of liturgical formation: preaching and hymn singing that drew him into a faith that was intentionally trinitarian.

What Ambrose and Augustine give us, together, is an appreciation that the Trinity serves as a template for the whole of the Christian life, and particularly for the interior life: the Father as the Source, the Son as the Mediator, and the Spirit as the one who unites and draws the whole of creation into fellowship with Father, Son, and Spirit.

CONCLUSION

Much more could be said about what the church in an increasingly secular society might learn from the early church. For example, the two Western voices explored in this chapter could be complemented by the equal and powerful trinitarian emphasis from the East, and we are witnessing today a major renewal of interest in a variety of early church voices.[24] I have chosen to highlight three things in particular—not to be

---

[24]Many contemporary voices are finding fresh and valuable insight by leaning more extensively into the Eastern fathers: see Michael Paul Gama, *Theosis: Patristic Remedy for Evangelical Yearning at the Close of the Modern Age* (Eugene, OR: Wipf & Stock, 2017), along with the magisterial work of Sarah Coakley, *God, Sexuality, and the Self: An Essay "on the Trinity"* (Cambridge: Cambridge University Press, 2013). See also Coakley, ed., *Re-Thinking Gregory of Nyssa* (Malden, MA:

exhaustive, of course, but to demonstrate at the very least that the pre-Christendom church is an invaluable resource to the church today.

First, we learn much from the pre-Christendom church about how to engage in the public square, especially the principles of engagement without pandering, engagement while sustaining the capacity to speak truth to power, and engagement that seeks the common or civic good.

Second, we learn more about the crucial process of initiation into the Christian faith and incorporation into a distinctive community, with particular reference to the catechumenate.

And third, we learn how essential it is that we would cultivate an intentional interiority whose contours and character is shaped by the vision of a triune God. It is a trinitarian spirituality that is cultivated by and through the preaching and liturgical life of the church.

Blackwell, 2003). When it comes to questions of catechesis and Christian initiation, mention should be made of Gordon Miloski, *Baptism and Christian Identity: Teaching in the Triune Name* (Grand Rapids, MI: Eerdmans, 2009); Miloski also draws on the wisdom of Gregory of Nyssa.

5

LEARNING FROM HISTORIC MINORITY CHURCHES

WHILE THE CHURCH IN THE WEST is facing a relatively new phenomenon—the loss of voice and a privileged place in society—the church has always been a minority presence somewhere, and it has learned to thrive in such contexts. Some of these contexts—such as Japan, China, and India—have had a Christian presence that goes back many centuries, largely the fruit of Western missionary efforts. Others are truly ancient in that there has been a Christian presence in Lebanon, the Palestinian Territories, and Egypt that goes back to the second century.

For the purposes of this chapter, I will distinguish these Christian communities from the church in postcolonial Latin America and Africa. The church in the West has a great deal to learn from African and Latin American Christians, of course. But here I want to focus on what I would call "historic" churches, where the Christian community has been a minority presence for centuries if not actually millennia.

The church in Japan, China, India, and Egypt has always had a theological and missional vision for what it means to be the church. Yet those in the West have not always recognized and appreciated this contribution, and indeed we have often assumed that the "center" for theological reflection and what it means to be the church in mission has been cultivated in the West. Now any such assumption needs to be set aside; those in the West should rather engage these voices as peers, if not actually as senior voices within the global Christian community. After all, they have been wrestling with what it means to be a minority presence for centuries. The Christian community in an increasingly pluralist and secular context can learn a lot from historic minority churches about what it means to flourish and witness to the reign of Christ from this minority position.

I know it is audacious and perhaps presumptuous to put voices all the way from Japan to Lebanon under a single category. There is a huge diversity of opinion among historic minority churches, and those in China may well respond to their challenges in a very different manner to those in Egypt. In China, there is both the government recognized church and the house church movement; each represents a different approach to what it means to be a minority Christian presence and voice. Indeed, surely part of learning what it means to thrive in a secular context might very well come from attending to the *diversity* that comes from these distinct voices.

In spite of this diversity, though, we can identify distinctive themes that arise out of the phenomenon of being a minority Christian presence. Each of these perspectives is a source of potential encouragement to the church in an increasingly secular context. They demonstrate in three particular ways that the church can thrive and be true to its identity and mission from such a social and cultural position.

CHRISTIANITY AND THE "RELIGIONS"

First, a major theme for historic minority churches is what it means to be the church in the context of the dominant religion of the society, such as Hinduism in India, Buddhism in Japan, and Islam in Egypt. One helpful voice is that of Martin Accad, who writes from the experience of the Christian community in Lebanon.[1] He speaks of the need, as he puts it, to "deminoritize." He means not that we deny that we are a minority but rather that we have to get past the idea that we are somehow oppressed victims, and thus continually on the defensive. We need to recover a vision that as a remnant we are called to be a blessing to the nations.

Once we have moved beyond the notion that we are an oppressed minority, we can then, as Accad puts it, "deradicalize" our perception of

---

[1]The comments that follow arise from Accad's essay "Theological Education as Formation for Prophetic Ministry," https://abtslebanon.org/imes-blog/2017/03/02/theological-education-as-formation-for-prophetic-ministry.

the other—that is, we choose to take a generous posture toward the majority. We do not hold a stereotypical view of the other as threat, with ourselves as passive victims. In Accad's Lebanese context, the church comes to see Muslim neighbors as "potential partners in the betterment of society." This posture is only possible if we can always remember that we exist as the church not for our own sake, but for the sake of the world; we develop an "alternative consciousness" in which we see ourselves as called to be salt and light. A good and accessible resource on this topic is Ajith Fernando's *Sharing the Truth in Love: How to Relate to People of Other Faiths*.[2] He writes out of the context of the Christian community in Sri Lanka. In his book, Fernando emphasizes two primary themes: the need for humility and the need for shared learning. To these I would add the need to learn how to work with those of other faiths in seeking the common good.

For the Christian in a pluralist and secular context, deradicalizing means that we have a generous disposition toward our Muslim or Hindu neighbor. But more, it also means that we ask how secularity is not so much a threat where we are the victim, but a context that may present new and distinct opportunities to be salt and light.

In a fascinating essay published in *Christianity Today*, Sunday Bobai Agang notes that it is common for the church in Nigeria to speak of the threat of a radical Islamic agenda. Without downplaying the problem that exists with radical Islam, he goes on to stress that this threat is overblown and that it distracts the church from the real threat, which is *internal*: the moral and ethical collapse of the Christian community, shown in the lack of integrity in their business dealings and the lack of an ethical witness in the public square. He notes the inconsistency of public acts of religiosity and a lack of an ethical or moral compass, and observes: "These matters are more lethal to the Christian faith than any Islamization agenda."[3]

Similarly, we need to challenge the assumption that the great threat to the church in the West is secularity, which, some assume, has opened the

---

[2]Ajith Fernando, *Sharing the Truth in Love: How to Relate to People of Other Faiths* (Grand Rapids, MI: Discovery House, 2014).

[3]Sunday Bobai Agang, "Radical Islam Is Not the Nigerian Church's Greatest Threat," *Christianity Today*, May 2017, 56.

door to radical Islam. This too is an overblown description of a false threat to the church. To the contrary, we might discover that secularity opens up new opportunities to the church and, in turn, the church might actually welcome Muslim immigration.

When theology is truly indigenous and truly contextual, the church looks for opportunities that arise because of the encounter with other religious traditions, including secularity. We look for ways to open up new vistas of learning and witness, and for ways to foster distinctive expressions of Christian identity. A Christian faith that is truly Chinese, for example, would incorporate distinctly Chinese religious sensibilities. C. S. Song is a premier Chinese theologian of the last century who has intentionally drawn on Buddhist and Confucian sources of wisdom and spirituality to articulate what it means to think and act Christianly in that context.[4] This has also been a major focus of conversation for theologians in India as they ask whether a person can maintain their "Hindu" identity—which is so much a part of what it means to be Indian—and still be a Christian. Is it possible to remain culturally integrated, to be a "Hindu" follower of Christ? Of course, there is a powerful and substantial discontinuity between Hindu sensibilities and Christian experience, yet there might also be striking points of continuity.

Some no doubt have gone too far in identifying points of continuity. The Catholic theologian Raimon Panikkar was intentionally syncretistic as he sought what might be called a Hinduized Christianity. Yet others have insisted rightly that we can sustain the integrity and distinctiveness of the Christian faith while also drawing on the spiritual sensitivities and practices of the majority religion, whether these be Hindu or Buddhist, incorporating them into Christian worship and spiritual practices. Why, for example, would a church building in India look so much like a church in Western Europe rather than a Hindu temple? Why would a church in Lebanon be a replica of a church in the United States? Why should it not be closer in its design to the mosque down the street?

Paul Sudharkar and R. C. Das have claimed that Christian faith is the fulfillment of Hindu aspirations. If this is the case, nothing is gained by

---

[4]C. S. Song has a number of significant publications, but a good place to begin might be *Tell Us Our Names: Story Theology from an Asian Perspective* (Maryknoll, NY: Orbis Books, 1984).

demonizing Hinduism. Rather, we may speak to the good, the noble, the very legitimate that is found within it. Perhaps the same could be said for secularity: there may be something in the secularity of the West that is actually a good thing, something that the Christian community can affirm and actually build on. Rather than demonizing the secular, we could begin to demonstrate that people who are truly secular might in time come to see that their deepest aspirations and longings are found in Christ. If we are careful to distinguish *secularity* from the ideology of *secularism*, it might provide the church in the West a point of both learning and opportunity.

Complicating the relationship with the dominant religion of society is that the historic minority church often faces the charge that Christianity is a foreign religion. It is assumed, for example, that to be Pakistani is to be Muslim. And not only that, but if you are not a Muslim Turk (to take another example), you are a threat to what it means to be truly Turkish. In many contexts, Christianity is viewed as an import from the West and a threat to national identity. Historic minority churches often have to make the case that Christianity is not "foreign."

Make no mistake: Christianity will always be a threat to national identity on some level. Sunday worship is a profoundly political act in that it makes clear that allegiance is no longer local or national; there is no other God but the Creator, who is necessarily a threat to "Caesar." But even given this ultimate allegiance, why should the church not strive to show how the Christian faith is not an immediate threat to what it means to be Chinese, or Lebanese, or Canadian? We must demonstrate that our ultimate allegiance is elsewhere—on this there is no compromise. And yet, on so many points, our lives as Christians arise from and are informed by the very best of our religious and secular context. When, for example, Americans assume that to be truly American is to be secular, surely our response should *not* be to insist that "America is a Christian country," but rather to show that Christian communities can accept the secular context and work with the possibilities and opportunities that this creates.

All this means it is important that those who give leadership to the church in a secular context are conversant with both the religious communities with which they share the public square and with the dominant "religion" or ideology of the society—secularity—even as a church leader in Egypt needs to be familiar with Islam and a church leader in Japan should know Buddhism well. When I was a seminary student in the 1970s, only those of us who anticipated some form of international ministry were expected to be conversant with other major religious traditions. Now all of those called into leadership for the church in the West should have a working knowledge of the diverse religious traditions of their neighbors, as well as of secularity, in order to leverage the possibilities that arise from this social, cultural, and political reality.

Christian experience and reflection in the pluralist and secular West will still look different from the experience of the church in India, and rightly so. Even as churches in the global South had to learn how to contextualize their faith and not merely import their theology from the West, now those theological voices from the global South can call the church in the secular West to do precisely the same: contextualize the faith for this time and this place.

So what might it mean for the church to be open to new perspectives— not demonizing, but attending to the good in the dominant religious or ideological presence? Of interest here is the experience of the church in China, which faces the hegemony of a state and atheistic regime. Here, one might think, there is no positive on which the church can build. Yet still we can look to those who witness to human aspirations. For example, Xiaoli Yang, an emerging Chinese theologian, has chosen to give particular focus to the poetry of Haizi.[5] Haizi tragically took his own life in 1989 at twenty-five, but his life and poetry have resonated deeply with a significant cross-section of the Chinese population. In particular, he very much captures the longings and sensibilities of the Chinese people after the 1989 Tiananmen Square incident. Yang observes that his suicide and poetry are part of a distinct social and cultural movement or awareness. What emerges in Haizi's poetry is a particular longing for home—and the journey or path *toward* home.

---

[5]Xiaoli Yang, *A Dialogue Between Haizi's Poetry and the Gospel of Luke: Chinese Homecoming and the Relationship with Jesus Christ* (Boston: Brill, 2018).

Yang engages Haizi's poetry through the lens of the Gospel of Luke, observing that this longing for home resonates with this Gospel, including such themes as moving from alienation (homelessness) into the enlarged home of God's presence in the world, moving toward table fellowship, and moving from brokenness to reconciliation. All of this happens through the radical vulnerability of God, whose hospitality and suffering connect deeply with the experience of the Chinese people. The response must be one of surrender—again, a theme that is present in Haizi's poetry and in the Gospel as well. Thus, Yang concludes:

> God's revelation in the gospel is like a diamond, reflecting its beauty in different dimensions through various cultures. By the truth encounter of the other, each party in a dialogue is invited to wonder at the grace and beauty of God as they appear in Haizi's poetry and Luke's Gospel. As Luke discovers the Kingdom of God brought by Jesus in light of the Easter event, this book demonstrates also the Spirit's active presence in a generation of the post-Mao era, as reflected in Haizi's poetry. Within their deep-set yearnings and raw expressions, the Spirit is not antagonistic to using imperfect human cultural artefacts to begin this process of revelation.[6]

The fruitfulness of Yang's engagement with Haizi should cause us to wonder, if we are going to give leadership to the church in a secular age, whether we should attend more to the poets of our times. Could it be that in reading the poets—not just religious poets—we will be able to get past the distraction of our age and find a way to attend to the inner sensibilities of the human soul in this time and in this place? Attending to the good in our religious or ideological context is to attend to what Yang speaks of as the "deep-set yearnings and raw expressions" of the culture. These, she suggests, are the evidence of the Spirit's active presence in our generation.

CULTURAL AND POLITICAL ENGAGEMENT

Related to sustaining the faith in the midst of the dominant religions and ideologies, those from the minority Christian world also call us to

---

[6]Yang, *Dialogue*, 289.

develop what is typically called "public theology": theology that leads to practice and engagement with diverse social and cultural constituencies. This helps us attend to the question of what it means to be genuinely and sincerely political.

Andrea Z. Stephanous, writing from Egypt, observes that the church tends to respond in two ways to his social, cultural, and political context. Some choose to withdraw and, as he puts it, "form isolated islands apart from the surrounding community in order to avoid the danger of disintegration of their religious identity and their fusion with the Muslim majority." Others go the other direction and adopt the "sayings and concepts of political Islam as a form of political nationalism."[7]

Stephanous contends that the better alternative is to develop a distinctive Arab thought—a unique and particular way of thinking—as the ideological basis for political and cultural engagement. This presumes that it is not only possible but essential that we affirm the positive values of our social context and then also seek to benefit the society as a whole, not just our particular religious group.[8]

Thus, following Stephanous, we need to resist the temptation to privatize religion and instead insist, first, that a religious perspective is essential to public discourse. This means, of course, that the church needs to defend the right of a religious voice in the public square, but also that we need to learn how to effectively speak with that voice. Second, if indeed the gospel has public implications, we need to develop a *public* theology, keeping in mind Stephanous's insistence that public theology has no credibility without active advocacy for and commitment to social justice.[9]

Corneliu Constantineanu addresses the same question from the perspective of the minority evangelical and pentecostal churches of Romania, particularly with reference to what it meant to be the church within the context of a communist regime. He notes, as Stephanous does, that there is the temptation to retreat—to privatize religion. Under the communist regime, churches either withdrew from society or

---

[7]A. Z. Stephanous, "Middle Eastern and Arab Theology," in William A. Dyrness and Veli-Matti Kärkkäinen, *Global Dictionary of Theology* (Downers Grove, IL: IVP Academic, 2008), 539.

[8]Stephanous, "Middle Eastern and Arab Theology," 539.

[9]Stephanous, "Middle Eastern and Arab Theology," 539.

"collaborated with the communist authorities conceding to their imposed limitations on churches."[10] The result was that the churches believed that the only option was to keep their heads down and their faith private. If they did, they could live apart from the broader society and perhaps do just fine, such that their faith had little if anything to do with the social, cultural, and political world in which they were located.

Yet Constantineanu insists that it is essential that Christians engage meaningfully in the public domain and seek to influence policy and social structures. He also calls for a public theology, calling it "a serious engagement of the Christian faith with the public domain in all its social, political, cultural, and economic spheres of life in society."[11]

Constantineanu emphasizes, though, that not just any kind of public witness is legitimate or effective. Political witness needs to be marked by "hope, compassion, reconciliation, and social healing."[12] Christians begin with the assumption that the gospel has something to offer the common good and then learn the skills or capacities for navigating and bringing wisdom into the public square. However, we need to graciously accept both the potential but also the limitations of that contribution— meaning, of course, that we learn what it means to be in dialogue with those with whom there are real differences.[13] In all of this, we are seeking the common good; we are not just looking out for the good of the Christian community.

Is this kind of public theology possible? For Constantineanu, the only real threat to the church is fear. Fear and anxiety annihilate our capacity to imagine and envision the future into which we are called.[14]

THE SUFFERING CHURCH

Finally, historic minority churches can teach the Western church what it means to be a suffering church. Christians in the West have, on the whole,

---

[10]Corneliu Constantineanu, "God in Public: A Prolegomena to Public Theology in the Romanian Context," *Journal of Humanistic and Social Studies* 8.1 (15) (2017): 168.

[11]Constantineanu, "God in Public," 168.

[12]Constantineanu, "God in Public," 171.

[13]Constantineanu, "God in Public," 172-73.

[14]Corneliu Constantineanu, "Theology for Life: Doing Public Theology in Romania," *Journal of Humanistic and Social Sciences*, 8.2 (16) (2017): 99.

not experienced persecution—though perhaps I need to be more specific and speak of Christians who are descended from northern European settlers. African American, indigenous, Italian Catholic, and other minority Christians have experienced persecution.

For a long time, more privileged Christians have had a direct influence on political and social levers of power in the West. This has resulted in a society that has sustained freedom of religion and permitted the church to go about its worship and ministry with little if any interference. Indeed, the northern-European-descendant church in the West has taken for granted that the state supports Christian communities and does not interfere or significantly limit their practices. Very few, if any, have suffered for their faith, other than perhaps converts from other religious traditions who have been ostracized from their family of origin.

It is not so in countries where Christians are a historic minority, such as Japan. To get insight into this experience, Christians in the West might consider reading *Silence*, a novel by Japanese Christian author Shusaku Endo that was made into a 2016 film by Martin Scorsese. The historical novel wrestles with the question of not just persecution but apostasy in seventeenth-century Japan. It seeks to capture the genuine suffering of Japanese Christians in that era, along with the young Spanish Jesuit priest who came to Japan to assess whether apostasy had occurred.[15]

In Pakistan, Asia Bibi was finally released in November 2018 after eight years in detention for blasphemy against the Qur'an, including a year with a death sentence. While perhaps she made an unfortunate comment about the Qur'an, her experience points out the danger of blasphemy laws that are a constant threat to anything that Christians might say about Islam.

Take also Algeria, which had a substantial Christian presence until the 1960s, when the country went through significant upheaval. At first, this social revolution was secular in its orientation. But it soon morphed into an Islamic political movement, and in time militant groups like the

---

[15]My son, Micah D. Smith, read an early draft of this book and in response to this paragraph wrote: "Having read [*Silence*], I'm not sure I'd recommend it to many of the people who don't understand the experience of the minority church. It would be too much too fast!!! Maybe *The Mission* first, [a] movie with Jeremy Irons; then *Silence*."

Armed Islamic Group (GIA) began to target Christians. Many Christians fled the country, but some stayed. Many of these paid with their lives, including the seven monks of the Abbey of Our Lady of Atlas in Tibhirine. As Philip Jenkins writes, the monks' mission and vision for their monastery was to serve their Muslim neighbors. This was their vocation, including the giving of medical services.[16] They were martyred in 1996, and their story is presented in the 2010 film *Of Gods and Men*.

To gain insight into the church in China, Western Christians might read Liao Yiwu's book *God Is Red*.[17] For this fascinating piece of journalism, Liao traveled throughout China and interviewed laypersons and clergy. One of them, Sister Zhang Yinxian, was a nun who lived to over one hundred years old and persisted with extraordinary courage and determination to sustain a church, an orphanage, and a monastery in the face of an atheistic Communist regime. Here is Liao's description of his first encounter with her: "Zhang Yinxian was fast for someone who was more than a hundred years old, and as I caught up with her in the churchyard in the old section of Dali, it occurred to me that she looked every bit like a piece of fresh ginseng, slightly crooked but full of life and energy."[18] Her church was first closed in 1952, but then through persistence and dogged protests was reopened in the 1980s. In the meantime, the community witnessed the execution of a visiting Swedish priest.

There are many more potential examples, but the point is that for these Christian communities—in Japan, Pakistan, Algeria, and China—persecution and suffering have been and are an integral and assumed part of their Christian identity and experience. They are not surprised by it, and have learned to develop a theological vision for navigating these challenging circumstances with grace, hope, and perseverance. Far from being triumphalist, they know what it means to identify with the crucified God and with the suffering of the world. They are churches for which the word *martyr* is not just a reference to second-century Christians but someone whom they might have known personally.

---

[16]Philip Jenkins, "Algeria's Remaining Christians," *Christian Century*, March 13, 2019, 44-45.

[17]Liao Yiwu, *God Is Red: The Secret Story of How Christianity Survived and Flourished in Communist China*, trans. Wen Huang (New York: HarperOne, 2011).

[18]Liao, *God Is Red*, 11.

Additionally, we see in these historic minority churches an appreciation that God is on the side of the marginalized and oppressed. The two—suffering for one's faith and identification with those who suffer as the poor—go together. It is often the case that the suffering of the church is *occasioned* by the insistence that it will defend the cause of the refugee, the orphan, and the widow. J. Scott Jackson makes this point in his review of a theological biography of Oscar Romero, the Catholic archbishop of San Salvador who was murdered while celebrating mass on March 24, 1980.[19] Romero grated on those in power because he was continually advocating for the poor and denouncing the state-sponsored terrorism of the very paramilitary death squads that eventually came to his door. Romero rejected all forms of violence, including retribution, and insisted that the mission of the church must include a radical identification with those who suffer at the hands of those in power. As Jackson notes, perhaps in our day we need to revise our definition of *martyr* from only focusing on those who are hated for affirming Christian faith to also include those who are hated because they identify with the oppressed.

When the church embraces suffering with the oppressed, many in the wider society take notice. On the thirty-year anniversary of the 1989 Tiananmen Square tragedy, Nathan Vanderklippe documented how the Chinese regime has sought to suppress all forms of religious expression, yet the number of Christians in China continues to grow. Though the Tiananmen protests were religiously agnostic, something shifted with their suppression. There emerged a growing disillusionment with what Vanderklippe speaks of as "the absence of belief," and this has led to a resurgence of spiritualities. He notes that many of the key leaders in the house church movement today came to faith after 1989. Four of the key leaders most sought by the state because of their leadership at the Tiananmen protests have since become Christians. Christian faith has become attractive and credible precisely because it supports the human rights that were suppressed in 1989. Intriguingly, 15 percent of those who were jailed and tortured in 2015 for their involvement in human rights

---

[19]J. Scott Jackson, "In Review: Oscar Romero's Political Theology [a review of *Revolutionary Saint: The Theological Legacy of Oscar Romero*, by Michael E. Lee]," *Christian Century*, October 10, 2018, 36-37.

advocacy were Christians. Vanderklippe concludes, quoting a Chinese scholar: "These lawyers choose to believe in God out of a sense of justice." The person he quotes, a Mr. Liu, was himself baptized only six months after Tiananmen.[20]

As the story of China post-Tiananmen makes clear, not only must the Western church learn from historic minority churches how to navigate the world of suffering and persecution itself, but that the suffering church is uniquely positioned to advocate for those who suffer at the expense of unjust regimes or systems. To be the suffering church requires a theological orientation that provides the intellectual and affective resources for navigating a world of suffering and even martyrdom. We need to gain an appreciation of what Japanese theologian Kazoh Kitamori speaks of in his book *The Theology of the Pain of God*.[21] We need to have a theology that accounts for suffering and, in particular, that shows us what it means that the church identifies with the suffering of God in Christ (Romans 8:17).

We need also to learn from these minority churches that the cross of Christ is not merely about God doing something about our guilt and sin. The cross is also a demonstration of the power of God to defeat evil. This means that biblical apocalyptic literature—Daniel and Revelation, for example—is not primarily about trying to figure out the "end times." Rather, these texts empower the church to live through darkness and difficulty with a deepening confidence that Christ is on the throne of the universe and that good will, ultimately, triumph over evil. The book of Revelation only makes sense when we see that it was written for and needs to be read through the lens of a suffering church.

CONCLUSION

In an exquisite sermon on the book of Daniel, Munther Isaac—Palestinian Christian and professor at Bethlehem Bible College—speaks to how Daniel 3 provides a vision for what it means to be the church when the church is a minority presence and an oppressed community. As Isaac puts it, the Christian community in Bethlehem is doubly a minority by

---

[20]Nathan Vanderklippe, "Tiananmen Protests Led to a Religious Revival," *The Globe and Mail*, June 1, 2019, A13.

[21]Kazoh Kitamori, *The Theology of the Pain of God* (Richmond, VA: John Knox Press, 1965).

being in a territory that is occupied by Israel and that has a majority Muslim population.[22] His conclusion is simply this: to navigate this situation requires courage, wisdom, and love. These three remain the abiding call to the church as it lives out its faith as a minority presence.

---

[22]Munther Isaac, "World Assembly 2015: 25 July, Munther Isaac, Daniel 3," IFES World, uploaded August 7, 2015, www.youtube.com/watch?v=LVCb3oIdc9Q.

6

CHRISTIAN VOICES FROM
SECULAR EUROPE

A FOURTH SOURCE OF LEARNING for the church in North America, New Zealand, Australia, and others along the path of secularization is the experience of the church in Central and Western Europe. While secularization may not proceed along a simple trajectory, as mentioned in chapter 1, we may still ask what the church in these regions that are coming into secularity later on can learn from those who have wrestled with what it means to be the church in a secular context and ethos.

As with the other three sources of learning, there is not a direct parallel between the two situations. A crucial difference is the phenomenon of the established, state church. European settlers, when founding the United States, insisted on a separation of church and state. Now, it is important to remember that in Europe there was always an "alternate church" separate from the state churches. There were Moravian and Baptist and Methodist movements in Germany and England, for example, that insisted that Christian faith was voluntary. They evangelized those who were Christian in name only and typically practiced believer's baptism. Nevertheless, there is a difference—but despite this difference, Christians in the new world have much to learn from Central and Western Europe.

There is diversity of opinion on what it means to be the church in a post-Christian era, but certain voices are simply indispensable. Søren Kierkegaard is in many respects the primary one. If you read no one else, read Kierkegaard, starting with *This Present Age*, then *Either/Or* and *Fear and Trembling*, followed by his fascinating essays on Christian spirituality, including *Purity of Heart Is to Will One Thing* and *Training in Christianity*. Then there are G. K. Chesterton, Karl Barth, and Jürgen

Moltmann. Three more contemporary perspectives that will be further referenced later in this book are Rowan Williams, the former Archbishop of Canterbury; Sarah Coakley, now professor emeritus of Cambridge University; and Tomáš Halík, writing from the perspective of the Catholic Church in the Czech Republic.

But in this chapter I will focus on three voices from post-Christian Europe:

- Dietrich Bonhoeffer, Lutheran theologian and pastor, is increasingly recognized as perhaps the most astute observer of the power of secularism of his generation. His work is more relevant than ever.

- Jacques Ellul, French lawyer, scholar, and churchman, was and remains a brilliant and astute observer of the rise of secularity in Europe from outside the established church.

- Lesslie Newbigin, the premier missiologist of his generation, is unique for his dual perspective having served in both India and in the United Kingdom.

These three were very close in age, born within six years of each other. Part of the intrigue in reading them together is seeing overlapping themes and complementary perspectives as they tried to make sense of growing secularity in Europe in the 1930s, the emerging crisis of National Socialism in Germany, and the Second World War. They did not always agree, and yet in reading them together they correct or amend each other. Ellul, for example, does not have a fully formed ecclesiology, but that is more than made up for in reading Newbigin and Bonhoeffer.

All insisted on the need to be in the world and engaged missionally with the world. They were not unaware of the world's deep fragmentation. What makes reading them so compelling is that they sustained a hopeful realism rather than a naive optimism. They wrestled like few others with what it meant to be Christian and the church during this period in Europe's history.

DIETRICH BONHOEFFER (1906–1945)

Dietrich Bonhoeffer's insights into what it means to be the church on mission have shaped the conversation like few others. Here I will stress three of his emphases that serve as very good reasons to be part of a

Bonhoeffer study group or to take a whole course on Bonhoeffer as part of one's theological formation.

Religionless Christianity. Bonhoeffer contended that the Renaissance was the turning point in the history of the West in one respect: after it, the church was no longer the defining authority in society that it had been. Society, culture, humanity could now, it was assumed, refuse the authority of the church and live without reference to God.

In a poignant letter to his colleague and friend Eberhard Bethge, Bonhoeffer asked a series of probing questions about what it meant to be the church in a "religionless age." Until then, the preaching and theology of the church had been "built on the 'religious a priori' in human beings."[1] But what does it mean if this a priori no longer exists as a basis for engagement with the other? What does a church, a congregation, a sermon, a liturgy, a Christian life, mean in a religionless world? How do we talk about God without religion—that is, without the temporally conditioned presuppositions of metaphysics, the inner life, and so on? How do we speak (or perhaps we can no longer even "speak" the way we used to) in a "worldly" way about God? In a religionless situation, what do ritual and prayer mean?[2]

Bonhoeffer proposed, and it is no less radical a thought now than it was then, that the church should actually *embrace* this new social, political, and cultural context. In his mind, the Christian community needs to accept that the world "has come of age" and then learn what it means to navigate this new world and thrive within it. For Bonhoeffer, secularity is providential and an opportunity for the church to grow up now that the social context and political system no longer will prop it up. This response is not seclusion or retreat but helps us learn what it means to be fully immersed in the world and—this is crucial—to identify with the suffering God who is very present to this world. Bonhoeffer teaches us how to *respond* rather than react to secularity—how to navigate this world with both wisdom and courage in a way that leverages this new reality rather than rejecting or fighting it.

---

[1]Dietrich Bonhoeffer, *Letters and Papers from Prison*, ed. John W. De Gruchy, trans. Isabel Best, Lisa E. Dahill, Reinhard Krauss, and Nancy Lukens, Dietrich Bonhoeffer Works 8 (Minneapolis: Fortress), 362.

[2]Bonhoeffer, *Letters and Papers from Prison*, 264-65.

The key point for Bonhoeffer is that we engage our world not from the posture of our religion—with our religious identity as the point of connection—but instead from the perspective of our shared humanity. He asked what form Christianity takes when we cannot presume any kind of religious identity or any shared religious assumptions. In other words, when we meet and engage our neighbor, the basis of our relationship is not whether they are part of our religious community. Our first question is not whether they are of our Christian faith. When it comes to public witness, the aim of the church is not so much to "please join our religion" as it is to call humanity to be fully human.

The meaning of church. Bonhoeffer did his doctoral studies at the University of Tübingen and his thesis, "Sanctorum Communio," focused on the structure of the church. He was convinced that the church was ill-prepared to meet the demands of a secular world and that, as a starting point, the church needed to rethink its own structure and form. This meant that he rejected any kind of sentimentality regarding the church; it was not merely a fellowship of like-minded Christians or merely a community of people who have found life in Christ. It was, rather, a community called into existence by God through the Word and the sacraments. But more, knowledge of Christ is fundamentally *ecclesial*; we know Christ and are in fellowship with Christ in and through the church. There is no separating Christ from the church.

At least two emphases came out of this work for him. First, ethics is fundamentally an ecclesial activity—that is, a Christian ethic is lived out first and foremost within the church. It is in the church *as* the church that people come to see and know themselves. This meant that Bonhoeffer questioned the legitimacy of the "state" church; he himself was part of what at that time was spoken of as the "confessing" church.

Second, we need structures that foster ecumenical engagement since the unity of the church is essential to its identity and mission. Bonhoeffer knew, on a very practical level, that the church in Germany could not face its challenges alone; it needed the resources and encouragement of the international Christian community. His involvement with the ecumenical movement started early when in 1931 he attended the gathering of the World Alliance for Promoting Friendship through the Churches in Cambridge, England. Ecumenism was for him a time to put aside what he called "outdated controversies, especially the interconfessional ones."[3] Sure, there were historical reasons for these divisions, but the church of his day needed to get beyond essentially inconsequential differences— real differences, perhaps, but not ones that could justify a lack of generous cooperation and shared witness.

Most extraordinary for his time, Bonhoeffer had a generous attitude toward the Roman Catholic Church. He visited Rome as a young man and was deeply moved by what he witnessed in the liturgical life of the Catholic parishes in Rome. While his primary ecumenical activity was with other Protestant denominations, it is striking that, as I will note below, his ecumenism was both theological and practical: he believed in the unity of the church, but he also recognized that his own community needed to draw on the encouragement and wisdom of other Christian communities, including the Roman Catholic Church, if it was to truly be a "confessing" church.[4]

Then also, over time Bonhoeffer came to see that the church has a political responsibility inherent in its mission—specifically in his case, in Germany, to fight not merely for democracy but for the very soul of Germany. The church is called to be the conscience of the state and to call the state to account. He was convinced that few things could so destroy the soul of the church as for it to allow itself to be a political tool of the state.[5] Bonhoeffer insisted that the church needed to retain its distance and sustain a prophetic role: calling the state to justice, alleviating the suffering of those who experience the injustice of the state, and taking direct political action when the state is failing to keep law and order.[6] In

---

[3]Bonhoeffer, *Letters and Papers from Prison*, 502.

[4]Bonhoeffer's generous disposition toward the Catholic Church led many, including Karl Barth, to wonder if he was trying to "catholicize" the Confessing Church. But Bonhoeffer was truly wanting to learn from the other. He remained a gentle critic of Catholicism; he felt that Catholic doctrine erred in confusing the church with the kingdom of God. And yet he was always the learner recognizing that there were resources in this tradition that were lacking within his own. Chapter 11 is devoted to ecumenism in a secular age, and in it I use Bonhoeffer as a primary reference.

[5]Dietrich Bonhoeffer, *No Rusty Swords: Letters, Lectures and Notes 1928–1936*, trans. John Bowden, ed. Edwin H. Robertson, Collected Works 1 (London: Collins, 1958), 157.

[6]Bonhoeffer, *No Rusty Swords*, 230.

other words, the church must be Christ "in the world," the hands and feet and voice of Christ: "The church is church only when it is there for others . . . and thus it must tell people in every calling . . . what a life with Christ is, what it means 'to be there for others.'"[7]

Finally, for Bonhoeffer the church in a secular age is a suffering church that participates in the suffering of God.[8] To be a Christian is not merely to participate in religious acts within Christian community; it must also mean a radical identification with the world—and this means suffering with and in the world. In other words, is it not merely that the church is persecuted but that it chooses intentionally to engage with and lament the deep fragmentation of the society in which the church is located.

Cultivating Christian identity. In the face of the extraordinary developments in Germany in the 1930s—the rise of the Nazi regime with the explicit support of the state church—Bonhoeffer saw that not only was there a need to establish a Confessing Church, but that this church needed to be thoroughly and intentionally Christian. Bonhoeffer believed there was such a thing as a false church, and thus there was a need to affirm and strengthen an authentic expression of the church in an alternate expression from the state church.

Yet it is important to stress that Bonhoeffer did not assume that this expression of the church was now a true church just because it was no longer a state church. The church is vulnerable to secularization either way—whether "state" or "confessing"—if the essential practices for sustaining a distinctive identity and ethic are not integrated into the life of the community.

Here we would do well to plumb the wisdom of his approach to theological and spiritual formation at Finkenwalde, the seminary that Bonhoeffer established for the Confessing Church. His book *Life Together*, one of the most important spiritual writings of the twentieth century, emerged from this experience. It is indispensable reading for anyone who would seek to give leadership to the church in a secular age.[9]

---

[7]Bonhoeffer, *Letters and Papers from Prison*, 503.

[8]Bonhoeffer, *Letters and Papers from Prison*, 361.

[9]Dietrich Bonhoeffer, *Life Together and Prayerbook of the Bible,* trans. Daniel W. Bloesch and James H. Burtness, Dietrich Bonhoeffer Works 5 (Minneapolis: Fortress, 1996).

As he went about shaping this alternative community, Bonhoeffer was well aware of the limitations of his theological and spiritual tradition. One of these was that the liturgy of the German Lutheran church was somewhat impoverished. Another was that the emphasis on grace within his tradition was one-dimensional and lacking in a genuine call to and practice of spiritual formation and discipleship. Bonhoeffer remained a Lutheran, but he was quite prepared to look elsewhere for the resources that were needed to cultivate a genuine expression of Christian community. As noted above, when Bonhoeffer visited Rome he saw Christian community in practice within another theological and spiritual tradition. This naturally informed his understanding of Christ and the church, but it also helped him to grow in an appreciation of spiritual practice and discipline. He recognized that the practices that sustain and nurture Christian identity were not so much Catholic as Christian, and that many of these practices were ancient. The rhythms of prayer, Bible study, and confession that perhaps came to him through more recent Catholic sources were actually monastic in origin.

Regardless of the source, Bonhoeffer called his Christian community to be a community of discipline and spiritual practice. Some have spoken of this as a new monasticism, but it is less a recovery and more an *adaptation* of Benedictine monasticism. Those in the Finkenwalde seminary were not monks; they were future pastors preparing to be in the world and bring the Word to the communities in which they would be serving. This was not the monasticism of seclusion from the world but of equipping for service in the world. This formation for being in the world required certain routines and rhythms—the means of grace that sustained a distinctive identity and interior vitality for Christian witness and service in a post-Christendom society. These perspectives and practices are essential if the church is going to genuinely be the church in a secular age.

The practices included, first, morning and evening prayer in community. In a letter to Karl Barth in 1936, Bonhoeffer noted that good theological work and leadership formation need to be located within a community marked by morning and evening prayer.[10] Second, the

---

[10]Dietrich Bonhoeffer, *Theological Education at Finkenwalde: 1935–1937*, trans. Douglas W. Scott Dietrich Bonhoeffer Works 14 (Minneapolis: Fortress, 1996), 254.

community was governed by word and sacrament, complemented by personal Bible reading and meditation. For Bonhoeffer the Psalms had pride of place—not surprising given the place that the Psalms played and play in the liturgical life of Christian monastic communities. Third, Finkenwalde was for Bonhoeffer a way to be truly the church and to preserve the future of the church by affirming the central place of *confession*. Life in Christian community is necessarily marked by mutual accountability that is exercised through the practice of confession.

More can and will be said about Bonhoeffer, but for now let us consider what the church in a secular society can learn from Jacques Ellul.

JACQUES ELLUL (1912–1994)

Jacques Ellul was one of the leading lay theologians of the twentieth century. By profession, he was a philosopher and sociologist who also taught law and economics at the University of Bordeaux. For a time he also served as the deputy mayor of Bordeaux. During the Second World War he was active in the French Resistance, and following the war vocally denounced the atrocities of the French military in the Algerian War. He came to faith in his late teens and throughout his life was active in his own church—the Reformed Church of France.

Theologically, some of Ellul's most significant works were his biblical studies, notably his expositions of the political dimensions of society in 2 Kings and the apocalyptic vision of the book of Revelation.[11] If you read nothing else by Ellul, read *Presence in the Modern World*, which is a cogent and accessible summary of the key themes of his contribution to the conversation about what it means to be Christian in a secular age. When we ask the question, What does theological formation and leadership look like in an increasingly secular world?, Ellul is an indispensable source of encouragement and wisdom.

The call to be in the world with a dual identity. Ellul insisted that the church is very much called to be in (but not of) the world. Whatever else he spoke to, he always came back to this: there is no escaping the world.

---

[11]Jacques Ellul, *Presence in the Modern World*, trans. Lisa Richmond (Eugene, OR: Cascade, 2016). For a good introduction to Ellul, see Jeffrey P. Greenman, Read Mercer Shuchardt, and Noah J. Toly, *Understanding Jacques Ellul* (Eugene, OR: Cascade, 2012).

We are enmeshed with the human reality and the human predicament. We cannot be above the world, somehow, or escape it. He opens *Presence in the Modern World* with this affirmation: "Scripture tells us that Christians are in the world and that there they should remain. Christians are not meant to be separate or to set themselves apart."[12]

Ellul did not offer these comments from afar; he was not a member of the clergy and did not write as one who is on the faculty of a theological seminary. Part of the genius of his perspective and his theology is that he was a layperson who lived and worked and wrote from within the world. This vantage point or social position comes through repeatedly in his work. As he himself puts it, "Our task, in effect, is to consider the layman's presence in the *world*, and not the part he plays within the Church."[13] When he speaks of how there is no escape from the sinful human predicament, he does so as one who sees and feels this intimately.[14]

Ellul echoes Augustine in speaking of two cities and insisting that we are citizens of both.[15] We are in the world, citizens of this world. But we do not belong to this world. We belong to another city. We have another master; we are citizens of another kingdom.[16] And what makes this challenging is that we have to live in both; we cannot abandon either. We are involved in the material history of this world, but our hearts belong to another. We live with this as a constant tension. Even though our ultimate loyalty is to another city, we are bound up with the economic and social context in which we are enmeshed—the earthly cities of which we are a part. Ellul himself was very much a part of the city of Bordeaux. He observed that while it was an accident of history that he was born in that city, it was very intentional for him to remain there and be thoroughly present there. He lived and worked within the warp and woof of Bordeaux and it was there, in that place, that he sought to live out this dual identity.

The discontinuity between the world and the kingdom of God. Despite his commitment to be in the world and to be a dual citizen, Ellul

---

[12]Ellul, *Presence*, 1.
[13]Ellul, *Presence*, 64.
[14]Ellul, *Presence*, 5.
[15]Ellul, *Presence*, 27-28.
[16]Ellul, *Presence*, 28.

recognized that there is a major contrast between the ways of the kingdom of God and the ways of the world. For Ellul, this disconnect is complete; they are in opposition to each other. When we live in the world, we are "living in the domain of the Prince of the world, of Satan, and all around us we constantly see the action of this Prince."[17] Nothing caught Ellul's attention about the "politics of man" or "the city of man" quite so much as the dependence on "technique": the allure of means over ends, of efficiency, of the emphasis on speed. Technology, as the means of the world, dehumanized one and all. Ellul spoke of the autocracy of means and the triumph of means.[18] We have become, for Ellul, a civilization of means.[19] Both the world and the Christian community are naive if they think that as long as the end is okay, the means are justified. We have become slaves of our means, and people have become workers—that is, our posture regarding persons is completely instrumental.[20] In contrast, for the Christian, means and ends must be held in unity; any "technique" has a bearing on the end. The means must be consistent with the end we seek—namely, the kingdom of God.

Even though Ellul was involved in the political life of his own city, he insisted that the church must at all costs avoid political entanglements. It is scandalous for the church to try to adapt, co-opt, or be party to political power—to "legitimize the state and to be an instrument of its propaganda."[21]. In particular, he noted the crisis of the German church endorsing National Socialism and the Russian Orthodox Church being used by Stalin for his propaganda. He grieved, in other words, when the church was so naive as to be "found in the process of justifying political power or action."[22]

---

[17]Ellul, *Presence*, 7-8.

[18]Ellul, *Presence*, 49. See also his insightful reflections on the text of 2 Kings in *The Politics of God and the Politics of Man*, trans. Geoffrey W. Bromiley (Grand Rapids, MI: Eerdmans, 1972).

[19]Ellul, *Presence*, 48.

[20]My own denomination identifies those who serve internationally as "international workers" in an attempt, it would seem, to no longer speak of them as "missionaries." And yet, one has to wonder if this reflects precisely the concern Ellul had about instrumentalist views of the human person.

[21]Jacques Ellul, *The Subversion of Christianity*, trans. Geoffrey W. Bromiley (Grand Rapids, MI: Eerdmans, 1986), 126.

[22]Ellul, *Subversion of Christianity*, 126.

By this he does not mean that the church is not invested in the civic square; it is rather that we must not "conform to the present age." As he puts it, "The scandal is that the church tries to use political power to ensure its own authority and to secure advantages."[23] The result is that the church becomes politicized.[24] Instead, he calls the church to be the church in the exercise of its voice, its influence, as a disavowal of the tools or "power" of the civic square. An individual Christian will serve in the political domain, but the church, as the church, must sustain a holy distance from the state and the ways of the state.

Nothing so captured the discontinuity between the kingdom of God and the sphere of our human life as Ellul's reflections on urban life. He wrote extensively and in depth on the city—most significantly in *The Meaning of the City*.[25] And Ellul did speak quite negatively about the urban phenomenon. While he affirmed that the city is the sphere of humanity's greatest achievements—the arts, government, law, and education—he maintained that nevertheless the city at its core represents the human aspiration for self-realization: self-sufficiency and human accomplishment apart from God. That is precisely what makes the city a threat to the kingdom of God. What Christians need to affirm again and again is that the only hope for the city is divine intervention—something to which the church must witness continually. We cannot fix the city; our only hope is to live faithfully and dependently on the revelation of God, and be deeply aware of the temptation to be sucked into the very means by which the city is built to try to redeem the city.

In the world as salt and light. Ellul does not discount the interior life or the importance of religious practice. However, his emphasis is elsewhere. He insists that the Christian life is lived out in the world—not as a mere abstraction, but as one—as he sought to be—who is concretely and tangibly present in the rough and tumble of daily life in the street. To be salt and light is to be within and enmeshed with the world.[26] It is not merely a matter of praying for the world, but being present in the

---

[23]Ellul, *Subversion of Christianity*, 127.
[24]Ellul, *Subversion of Christianity*, 129.
[25]Jacques Ellul, *The Meaning of the City*, trans. Dennis Pardee, (Eugene, OR: Wipf & Stock, 2003).
[26]Ellul, *Presence*, 2-3.

world. The kingdom of God is present as salt and light in the world through Christians who are intentionally living in the world.

However, as noted, he urges that we not have illusions that we can fix the world or transform the culture or make the society more Christian. We cannot make it better; for Ellul, it is doomed.[27] And yet we have no choice; we are called to be a sign of the kingdom of God and a means of grace. He writes:

> Thus we are caught between two necessities that form an unresolvable tension. On the one hand, we cannot make this world less sinful; on the other, we cannot accept it as it is. To reject either side is to reject the actual situation in which God has placed those whom he sends into the world. Just as we are caught in the tension between sin and grace, so also are we caught between these two contradictory demands. It is an infinitely painful position, it is very uncomfortable, but it is the only one that can be fruitful and faithful for the Christian's action and presence in the world.[28]

This is what he means when he says that we live with a tension and not an abstraction; we live in the concrete social, economic, and political realities of our context. And the point, to come back to what he has already stressed, is that the layperson feels this and lives this:

> When they live out this tension each day of their lives, their very presence leads the church to recognize the value and truth of the world's distress and leads the world to recognize its true problems beneath the lies that it strives to perpetuate so that it does not hear the Word of God. Thus the position of the layperson's life is essential for the church and for the world; it would be best therefore not to distort it.[29]

Yet this should not lead us to despair. Indeed, the Spirit is very much present in ordinary life, or, as he puts it, "in the entire course of God's action in history he uses a material medium, a human means, to act by his Spirit."[30]

---

[27]Ellul, *Presence*, 7.
[28]Ellul, *Presence*, 8.
[29]Ellul, *Presence*, 9.
[30]Ellul, *Presence*, 9.

For Ellul, *this* is the apologetic of the gospel—not arguments for the gospel but lives that are a living witness to the gospel.[31] This means that to be salt and light requires that Christians avoid human mechanisms of "power." In a fascinating argument, he insists that Christians must accept the power structures of the world along with all the limitations that this brings, but they need to avoid the use of power—notably political power—to achieve the kingdom of God. Ellul agrees that we must be about the preservation of the world, but he eschews aligning ourselves with political movements; this will always lead to a compromise of the church's witness. When speaking of what it means to be salt and light, Ellul suggests that the actions of the Christian are not "spectacular" but subtle: we learn to live at the margins, at the edges, not in absolute war, not in "direct attack" but by a more quiet but no less powerful witness.

Finally, in this regard, Ellul speaks to the work of the intellectual.[32] He recognizes that this calling, like all other occupations or vocations, needs to be oriented toward Christ and done in dependence on the illuminating work of the Spirit: "Whatever effort human beings have undertaken, its meaning and value have come only in Jesus Christ and by the Holy Spirit."[33]

Faith and hope in "an age of abandonment." In his writings, Ellul witnessed to the power of despair and cynicism and thus the indispensability of hope for the Christian. The genius of Ellul is precisely that he sustained hope in the midst of a very dark chapter in the history of Europe.[34] Hope, for Ellul, is ultimately nothing more than a confidence in God and in the coming of the kingdom of God. In this way, his hopefulness is deeply eschatological. In the end, he recognized that it is faith that sustains hope. More specifically, we have hope because of a faith that emerges from an attentiveness to divine revelation. Thus, faith is the

---

[31]Ellul, *Presence*, 10.

[32]Ellul devotes a whole chapter of *Presence in the Modern World* ("Communication") to the vocation of the intellectual. He speaks to the crucial role of the intellectual in the life of the church and society. It is a calling that brings one into the world of language, and language is all about building understanding with others, including those of other faiths.

[33]Ellul, *Presence*, 81.

[34]See Jacques Ellul, *Hope in Time of Abandonment*, trans. C. Edward Hopkin (New York: Seabury Press, 1973).

heart of the matter.[35] Without faith, we live by a pseudo-hopefulness—a naive optimism. And Ellul insists on a distinction between faith and belief—faith is not merely a matter of believing certain things to be true, but rather of a courageous and honest lived response to revelation. True faith is marked by an active presence in the world.

But more, Ellul observes that the Christian community is engaged in a spiritual battle, and thus prayer is essential to a Christian presence in the world. It is prayer that sustains our capacity to trust God to do what only God can do, and live with a resilient hope and confidence in the glorious return of Christ.[36] Hope is sustained by a prayerful dependence on the Spirit, who keeps our hearts and minds oriented toward the apocalyptic vision.[37]

LESSLIE NEWBIGIN (1909–1998)

Two of the potential sources of wisdom for the church in an increasingly secular "new world" are historic minority churches and the church in Central and Western Europe that is further along the path toward secularization. Lesslie Newbigin is unique in that he combined two of these; he spoke from the perspective of the secular West but did so after an extraordinary career in South Asia. In 1974, at age sixty-six, he returned to the United Kingdom and began to interpret the West in light of his experience in India. In so doing, he urged his Western contemporaries to do a fundamental rethinking of the character of the church and its mission.[38] When we read Newbigin, several themes emerge, four of which I will highlight here.

The nature of the church. First, Newbigin was well ahead of his time in his recognition that we can only engage a pluralist and secular society if

---

[35]Ellul, *Presence*, 10. For his more expanded reflections on faith, see Ellul, *Living Faith: Belief and Doubt in a Perilous World*, trans. Peter Heinegg (San Francisco: Harper & Row, 1983).

[36]Ellul, *Presence*, 31.

[37]See in particular his exposition of the book of Revelation, *Apocalypse: The Revelation of John* (New York: Seabury, 1977).

[38]The essential Newbigin reading list would include *Foolishness to the Greeks: The Gospel and Western Culture* (Grand Rapids, MI: Eerdmans, 1986); *Proper Confidence: Faith, Doubt, and Certainty in Christian Discipleship* (Grand Rapids, MI: Eerdmans, 1995); *The Gospel in a Pluralist Society* (Grand Rapids, MI: Eerdmans, 1989); and the much earlier contribution to ecclesiology that is the basis for all that follows in his writing: *The Household of God: Lectures on the Nature of the Church* (London: SCM Press, 1953).

we have clarity about what it means to be the church. As with Bonhoeffer, ecclesiology was foundational in Newbigin's writings. His groundbreaking and seminal study *The Household of God* was his first major theological contribution. He began with what it means to be the church, making a bold affirmation that may seem obvious now but altered the landscape at the time. He observed that in the history of the church there tend to be three distinct ways of conceiving of the church: catholic, with the emphasis on the sacraments; evangelical, with a focus on the Scriptures; and charismatic, with particular attention to the immediacy of the Spirit in the life of the community of faith. He contended that it makes no sense to pit these against each other; we need to affirm all three.[39] The church, to be the church, needed to be anchored within a sacramental tradition; it needed to be a community of the Word proclaimed and preached, and its existence was and is necessarily one that is sustained by a dynamic awareness of the presence and power of the Spirit. This is so because ultimately the church is one. For Newbigin, this meant that he worked tirelessly both in India and internationally to foster ecumenical relations.

The church as a sign of the kingdom. Second, Newbigin insisted that the church must focus its attention away from itself and instead sustain a dynamic vision of the reign of God. He confronted the so-called church growth movement, with its focus on survival and numbers rather than on the kingdom of God. The goal of the church is not the accumulation of members or numerical growth but to witness, in word and deed, to the kingdom. It is critical that we judge the effectiveness of a Christian community not based on its size or whether it is growing but instead on whether it truly is witnessing to the kingdom.

Thus, in what for many of his readers is his most important publication—*The Gospel in a Pluralist Society*—he spoke of the congregation as the *hermeneutic* of the gospel.[40] This always assumes an outward focus, as the church seeks to witness to the kingdom by the quality and character of its life and its service to the world. Fundamental to his conviction

---

[39]Many years later, as one who has learned so much from Newbigin, I published *Evangelical, Sacramental and Pentecostal: Why the Church Needs to Be All Three* (Downers Grove, IL: IVP Academic, 2017) with no other agenda than to keep current this insight and conviction about the church.

[40]Newbigin, *Gospel in a Pluralist Society*, 222-33.

about this witness to the kingdom is Newbigin's refusal to pit evangelism and social action against each other. Witness in word and deed presumes that both are essential and integral to the mission of the church: "They mutually reinforce and interpret one another. The words explain the deeds and the deeds validate the words."[41]

Public truth and the meaning of "confidence." For Newbigin, one of the great threats to the church was the rationalism of the Enlightenment. He was deeply concerned about the propensity of the church to buy into a rational apologetic for the faith. He insisted that knowledge is personal—not just facts or rational argument but *lived* truth. However, this does not mean that truth is private or merely personal. The gospel is public truth with cosmic implications, and specifically social, cultural, and political ones. He observed that in a pluralist society it is offensive to claim anything other than "personal" truth, but on this score we have no choice: the gospel is public truth. He insisted that while we can certainly affirm that pluralism is a fact of life, this does not mean that religious faith is an entirely private matter. If we confess Jesus Christ as Lord, we are making a public and political declaration. The early church suffered precisely because it declared that Jesus is Lord.

Having said that, he also insisted that the gospel is not a truth we possess; it is only a truth to which we witness. The One we serve is a servant king. Thus Newbigin calls for what he terms "proper confidence": a *humble* confidence in the unique authority of the risen Lord.[42] This means that we affirm the faith of the church, and do so knowing that this faith calls us to engage the social and cultural context in which we live with a commitment to speak the gospel and to be instruments of social and cultural transformation. Thus he insists, "Evangelism which is politically and ideologically naive, and social action which does not recognize the need for conversion from false gods to the living God, both fall short of what is required."[43]

The gospel and other religions. As noted, Newbigin wrote out of the experience of living and serving in South Asia as well as the United

---

[41]Newbigin, *Gospel in a Pluralist Society*, 137.
[42]Newbigin, *Proper Confidence*.
[43]Newbigin, *Gospel in a Pluralist Society*, 210.

Kingdom. Thus what he says about religion and the religions is particularly pertinent—echoing the perspective of others who speak from the vantage point of historic minority churches. He was insistent, for example, that there is truth in all religious traditions: "No person, of whatever kind of creed, is without some witness of God's grace in heart and conscience and reason, and none in whom that grace does not evoke some response—however feeble, fitful, and flawed."[44]

This conviction led Newbigin to two affirmations. First, that "we will expect, look for, and welcome all the signs of the grace of God at work in the lives of those who do not know Jesus as Lord."[45] We do not demonize the other; we do not speak of our neighbor in a way that discounts the work of the Spirit in them. And then, second, it also means that "Christians will be eager to cooperate with people of all faiths and ideologies in projects which are in line with the Christian's understanding of God's purpose in history."[46] This conviction means that, with the Jesus story as the defining witness to history that informs our lives and work, we can be in dialogue with those of other faiths, seeking common cause with them as we work toward the common good.

CONCLUSION

As this chapter comes to a close, three points about these perspectives from post-Christendom secular Europe merit emphasis. First, we learn from Bonhoeffer, Ellul, and Newbigin (and many others) that we need to find a way to coexist with secularity and actually thrive within a secular context. The appropriate response is not a militant, impulsive, or fundamentalist demonization of either secularity or Islam. We come to the public square with a gracious acceptance of the plurality of voices, recognizing that we are but one voice of many, looking for how the Spirit is present and calling us to be faithful in this context.

Second, we learn that in a secular context it is imperative that we foster a vibrant Christian maturity. This means that we must move beyond the propensity to foster a juvenile or sentimental religiosity that is nothing

---

[44]Newbigin, *Gospel in a Pluralist Society*, 175.
[45]Newbigin, *Gospel in a Pluralist Society*, 180.
[46]Newbigin, *Gospel in a Pluralist Society*, 181.

but an escape from the world rather than an empowerment for engagement with the world. We need an approach to liturgy and worship that is grounded in the ancient faith while also fostering the capacity for contemporary social and cultural awareness, evident at least in part in the capacity for lament.

And then, third, these voices are consistent in their assumption that the church cannot retreat from the world. It must sustain its identity while also learning what it means to live out the faith in the rough and tumble of political, economic, and social challenges—not with a privileged voice, but as one voice of many. This entails a willingness to, as needed, bear the pain of the world and carry the sufferings of Christ into this world. We do so, of course, by sustaining a vibrant and intentional faith that emerges from an active attentiveness to God's self-revelation.

7

FOUR CONTEMPORARY RESPONSES TO SECULARITY, PART 2

THE OPTIONS RECONSIDERED

IN CHAPTER 2, I identified four distinct responses to secularism:

- go along to get along

- monastic retreat and disengagement

- culture war

- redemptive engagement through faithful presence

Now that I have considered four sources of wisdom for the church in such a context, it would be appropriate to revisit these four options and consider them in light of these sources of wisdom. These sources of wisdom give us a way of seeing and considering these responses. They give us an interpretive grid by which we can assess the legitimacy of each of these ways of responding to secularity, including the strengths and limitations.

We need to be able to answer two questions about each response. First, Does this response to secularity foster the capacity of the church and individual Christians to foster a distinctive identity—one that is thoroughly and deeply Christian and consistent with the call of the Scriptures to be what it means to be the people of God? That is, does this response cultivate for the church and for the Christian a way of being that is consistent with the Christian theological and spiritual heritage?

And second, Does this response to secularity encourage and empower the church and individual Christians to be present in the world in a way that reflects the call of Scripture for the church to be a means of grace to and in the world as a witness to the reign of Christ? Another way to phrase this question is, Does this response to secularity foster the capacity of the church to be "in but not of" the culture and society in which it is situated? Does it help us to engage in mission, be faithful witnesses to the reign of Christ, and be present as salt and light? Are we engaged and present as those who have a distinctive and unique identity as the people of God?

As we evaluate the four responses noted in chapter 2, we will see that there are points of legitimacy to each but also aspects that might be a matter of concern—areas of limitation that could perhaps be addressed by one of the other three responses.

OPTION A: THE "GO ALONG TO GET ALONG" RESPONSE REVISITED

This is the posture that chooses to privatize religion, which is very much the expectation of a secular society. If we use the lens of "in but not of the world," this response seems to be clearly inadequate. On a fundamental level, we cannot accept the idea that faith must become entirely private and siloed. Christian identity must shape and inform our lives in the societies of which we are a part; our work in the world—in business, education, and the arts—will necessarily be deeply shaped by our Christian vision of work, vocation, and career. Christians cannot avoid— nor should they want to—the call of Christ to be salt and light, to be witnesses to the reign of God in word and deed. We are not called to the easy way; Christians need to be fully Christian even if that means there will be difficult times of conflict.

However, there is something in this perspective that merits affirmation. This response is at the very least not fighting the new social reality; it accepts that we live now in a secular world. There is, admittedly, something good—at least potentially good—in this. We do need to accept that we live in a pluralist and secular world and no longer insist that the Christian voice be privileged.

However, this is not an adequate response. Yes, we can accept that we now live in a secular age. And yes, we can perhaps see the benefits of secularity in the public square. But we cannot accept that religious life and practice are "private." Christian identity means not being of the world, and means being in the world in a way that truly reflects this identity and the purposes of God in the world.

This response could be thus easily dismissed, except that there may actually be a deeper problem afoot with the propensity to "just accept that we live in a secular world." The greater concern is that we then become inured to the sacred—that is, we silo our religious practices but we cannot silo our religious sensibilities. Could it be that by privatizing our faith and practice we live the bulk of our daily lives in a manner that is actually as secular as our agnostic or non-religious neighbor?

In *For the Life of the World*, Alexander Schmemann notes that there is a difference between secularism and atheism. The atheist, of course, utterly rejects the mere idea of God and the existence of the transcendent. In contrast, the secular person might well acknowledge that there is a God and affirm that there are God-given laws that should demarcate human life and work. The secular person, Schmemann observes, might well believe in life after death. Yet what is still missing is a sense of the sacred—the presence of transcendence in the world, and indeed in all of creation. Schmemann thus concludes that, despite the affirmation that God is there,

> All this changes nothing in the fundamental "secularity" of his vision of man and world, in the world being understood, experienced, and acted upon in its own immanent terms and for its own immanent sake. All this changes nothing in his fundamental rejection of "epiphany": the primordial intuition that everything in this world and the world itself not only have elsewhere the cause and principle of their existence, but are themselves the manifestation and presence of that elsewhere, and that this is indeed the life of their life, so that disconnected from that "epiphany" all is only darkness, absurdity, and death.[1]

This is reminiscent of deism—that, indeed God is there but God is so different and distant that the net result is that one lives one's life in the world no different from the one who denies the existence of God.

---

[1]Alexander Schmemann, *For the Life of the World: Sacraments and Orthodoxy* (Crestwood, NY: St. Vladimir's Seminary Press, 1998), 124.

OPTION B: THE MONASTIC RESPONSE REVISITED

The monastic response is to be commended in that it recognizes that the church could easily become unwittingly secular if it does not actively and intentionally establish the spiritual and religious practices by which an alternate way of life and community is cultivated. As noted, with Option A the danger is that the church would be inured to the context such that it loses its uniqueness. The church is no longer distinct, no longer sustaining a transcendent vision that then marks its common life and its shared identity. So, in one sense we can commend the monastic alternative in that refuses to be "of the world."

However, the monastic response is inadequate for at least two reasons. First, it fails to genuinely and effectively engage the world. We simply do not have the option of abandoning the world in which we are called to be present as salt and light. As noted in chapter 6, few have spoken to this as powerfully as Jacques Ellul. As Christians, we are called to be present to and active in the societies and communities in which we have been placed. Historic minority church communities have very often faced much more challenging circumstances than the church in the West, and they have demonstrated that we simply cannot abandon our call to engage our world in the name of Christ. We cannot choose the way of despair and cynicism about our world.

Second, the monastic alternative is also inadequate for the more complex reason that, while bemoaning the so-called decline of civilization, those of this persuasion have failed to see the way in which secularity opens up new possibilities for Christian identity and mission. The monastic alternative essentially gives up on society. But do we even have this as an option? Can we, before God, give up on our society and culture? More to the point, this giving up blinds us to a new context or situation that calls for a renewed form of being the church in the world.

Here is where the alternate vision of Augustine of Hippo, in contrast to Benedict of Nursia, is so relevant. James K. A. Smith leverages this Augustinian perspective in his response to Rod Dreher's book *The Benedict Option*. Dreher argues that we are living in a similar climate to Benedict, who concluded that the demise of Rome meant not only that there was nothing good in Rome but that it was impossible to sustain an authentic Christian witness in the midst of Rome. Dreher contends that the current political landscape is an impossible one for the Christian; it is a losing proposition to engage the public space and defend Christian virtues. With the decline of Christianity, we are facing the end of civilization as we know it—another "dark ages." Thus the only hope for the church is separation from the society at large. But Smith suggests that, rather than a "Benedict option," the church today should consider what he speaks of as the "Augustinian call."[2] Smith concludes with these comments:

> Dreher's Benedict is one option the church could take in the twenty-first century. As I argue in *Awaiting the King*, my hope is that instead we'll answer an Augustinian call: centering ourselves in the life-giving practices of the body of Christ, but from there leaning out boldly and hopefully into the world for the sake of our neighbours.

Yet there is wisdom in the monastic response; it cannot be entirely dismissed. Leaning into the wisdom of Dietrich Bonhoeffer, it is not an overstatement to say that the church will not truly engage the culture and society if it does not embrace practices of *dis-engagement*, practices that run against culture and that nurture a distinctive Christian identity. Bonhoeffer, echoing Kierkegaard's *Training in Christianity*, calls the church to those practices—essentially monastic practices—that cultivate this alternate identity. Could it be that the ancient rhythms of the monastic tradition are absolutely essential to cultivate the church's ability to be in the world but not of the world?

Perhaps we should consider the Francis or the Dominic "option." The genius of the mendicant orders, established by Saint Francis and Saint Dominic, is that they took monastic principles and practices and brought them into the very heart of the city. Rather than retreat, they established communities of faith that reflected many of the Benedictine practices and located these communities in the city as they sought to be a presence of gospel grace to the people there.

---

[2]James K. A. Smith, "The Benedict Option or the Augustinian Call?," *Comment*, March 6, 2017, www.cardus.ca/comment/article/the-benedict-option-or-the-augustinian-call.

Or we might go one step further and consider the approach of apostolic orders like the Jesuits and the Paulists. These Catholic religious orders are not monastic, but they sustain daily rhythms of prayer and spiritual practice. These practices inform their daily life but also their engagement in the world. Jesuits, for example, speak of "seeing God in all things" such that they are attentive to the ways in which God is actually present in society rather than bemoaning the ways in which God is, seemingly, not present. They see God in all things precisely because they sustain the practices of prayer and contemplation, adapted from ancient monastic routines and rhythms.

Here, too, I wonder about the place of what we might call an occasional or a temporary monasticism, thinking of the practice of retreat where we disengage from society for a season, getting away for everything from a weekend to a week or longer for a period of sabbath prayer and reflection. We do this as a way to cultivate our distinct identity, as a way to assure that we sustain the capacity to be discerning and not be consumed with the fear that pervades the culture all around us. In this case, retreat has a monastic quality to it, not as a permanent way of turning away from society but as a temporary distancing that renews and equips for genuine and discerning engagement.

I will speak more about this in the closing chapter of this book. For now, I will affirm that we will be consumed by our culture if we do not have practices—essentially monastic practices—that foster a distinct identity and disposition and, with this, the capacity for discernment and engagement with our world.

OPTION C: THE CULTURE WARS RESPONSE REVISITED

The "culture wars" response is that which, in effect, wants to turn the clock back. The assumption in this case is that the nation was once Christian and we need to restore that religious identity. As mentioned in chapter 2, this war is typically fought on three fronts: the courts, the schools, and the legislatures. Few have described this way of engagement with a secular society as effectively as has David Brooks:

> Many Christians notice that there are widening gaps between their values
> and secular values, especially in matters of sexuality. This can slip quickly

into a sense of collective victimhood. The "culture" is out to get us. We have to withdraw into the purity of our enclave. The odd thing is that the siege mentality feels kind of good to the people who grab on to it. It gives people a straightforward way to interpret the world—the noble us versus the powerful and sinful them. We have the innocence of victimhood.

Pretty soon Christianity isn't a humble faith; it's a fighting brigade in the culture war. "Evangelical" stops being an adjective and turns into a noun, a tribe. Pretty soon the ends justify the means—anything to defend the tribe. Pretty soon you get these wild generalizations about the supposed hostility of the outside world. . . . Pretty soon you wind up with what Rabbi Sacks calls "pathological dualism," a mentality that divides the world between those who are unimpeachably good and those who are irredeemably bad.[3]

Nothing is gained and much is lost when our approach is *adversarial* and when we are constantly choosing new battlegrounds to somehow keep a Christian privileged voice. It is a losing battle, and while fighting this losing battle we are missing out on the new opportunities that are being given to us for Christian witness and engagement. We live in a social and cultural context that calls for a new vision of what it means to be the church.

When I say it is a losing battle, what I mean is that perhaps we are called to appreciate that secularity is not the end of the world or of civilization. Perhaps we should come to see that secularity represents a new opportunity for Christian witness. If we do this, we will not fight it, and we will not continue to insist that the society is "Christian." We can accept that a nativity crèche is no longer outside city hall at Christmas time. We can accept that the Lord's Prayer is no longer said before city council meetings. Perhaps, indeed, we can actually go further and not presume that this Christian prayer would be used for public gatherings and actually take the lead on finding a more religiously neutral way to open these kinds of events. That is, there is a sense in which we do "go along to get along." We stop fighting the losing battle to keep our Christian privilege.

Not only is this a losing battle, but there is a particular danger to the culture wars approach: frequently, it comes across as an attempt to preserve

---

[3]David Brooks, *The Second Mountain: The Quest for a Moral Life* (New York: Random House, 2019), 256.

not merely Christian privilege but *white* privilege. From 2001 to 2004, Alabama had a debate about the placement of a Ten Commandments monument in the state supreme court. Former chief justice Roy Moore, who put the monument there, knew he had the support of the evangelical conservative Christian community. But as *Christianity Today* editor Mark Galli has so brilliantly observed, when Moore lost the Alabama Senate race in 2017, the biggest loser was the Christian faith and the reputation of the Christian community who so unwisely associated themselves with someone accused of racial and religious bigotry, misogyny, and sexual assaults.[4]

The grave danger with the culture wars approach is that the church, in an effort to keep society Christian, all too easily gets aligned with a particular political party. When this happens, the church loses its capacity to speak truth to power—to challenge the civic authorities with truth and the call to justice. We urgently need the reminder of Ambrose of Milan and Jacques Ellul that the church must sustain its independence from government and never lose its ability to challenge political leaders regardless of their party affiliation.

Yet there is also wisdom in the culture wars response. We can and must speak of how the Christian faith is countercultural. There is always a discontinuity between a secular society and the Christian faith. And each generation of Christians needs to see the points at which the church in its speaking, preaching, and teaching needs to challenge the cultural conventions and norms that are inconsistent with the reign of God. However, we need to choose our battles carefully and develop the political savvy to actually make a difference.

For example, the concern about abortion is legitimate. However, in making this a fault line between faith and culture, might we lose the capacity to provide genuine pastoral support and alternatives for those with unwanted pregnancies—offering hospitality and hope rather than condemnation and even potentially incarceration?

The concern about matters of human sexuality is likewise legitimate. But this has to be located in a broader ethic—a moral vision that is not

---

[4]Mark Galli, "The Biggest Loser in the Alabama Election," *Christianity Today*, December 12, 2017, www.christianitytoday.com/ct/2017/december-web-only/roy-moore-doug-jones-alabama -editorial.html.

reduced merely to matters of sexuality. We can legitimately ask whether this really is the primary battle to which the church is being called. Is this the hill that we will die on?

I would propose two hills that we should be prepared to die on. First, we have to sustain a deep commitment to pluralism. Rather than fighting to sustain Christian privilege, instead we should insist that society is best served when religious expression is not merely private but fully part of the social fabric and the public square. Thus we can speak of "principled pluralism," a posture that creates space for diversity of beliefs around a common commitment to civic well-being. We do not enforce belief, insisting on conformity, but neither do we deny the presence of deeply religious convictions.

This means that we also defend the voices of those of other ideological and religious persuasions. The public square should be a common space where diversity is both acknowledged and welcomed. Shapri D. LoMaglio states it well:

> Pluralism's great strength is that it does not ask people to weaken their beliefs, political or religious. In fact, it preserves a guaranteed space for them to hold those beliefs strongly—and to live them out in both their public and private lives. Consequently, there should be no greater champions for principled pluralism than Christians.[5]

This means that Christians can advocate for a political system that defends freedom of belief and conscience for all, including the Muslim, so that Christians themselves can nurture the vitality of their own faith. Secularity may then actually not be an enemy but instead provide a context in which the faith can flourish and the mission of the church can happen. However, we can only with integrity defend our own right to be thoroughly and deeply Christian and to have a voice in the public square if and as we grant that voice to others and defend their right to affirm their own faith and speak from the posture of that faith to the society at large.

---

[5]Shapri D. LoMaglio, "Our Commitment to Pluralism Should Not Waver," *Advance*, Spring 2018, 21. See also the very fine publication by John D. Inazu, *Confident Pluralism: Surviving and Thriving through Deep Difference* (Chicago: University of Chicago Press, 2016).

Second, we need to lean in to the wisdom and perspective of the exilic and postexilic prophets and appreciate the vital place of economic justice in the witness of the church. The perspectives of Lesslie Newbigin and the historic minority churches also remind us that worship and witness have no credibility without a commitment to economic justice. Isaiah 58 speaks of how worship is vacuous if it is not accompanied by active care for the poor, for the worker, and by implication for the immigrant and the refugee. So much contemporary evangelical worship seems escapist rather than empowering God's people to attend to the social and economic structures in which they live and work. Isaiah 58 suggests that this is deeply incongruous. We might here attend to Nicholas Wolterstorff's observation that for the Old Testament prophets there is no holiness without justice, and no justice without *economic* justice.[6] Frequently, our notions of holiness are limited to morality; while moral depth and integrity is essential, the prophets remind us that it is not a true morality if it is not reflected in a commitment to economic justice.

We must go further and address the deep racial and ethnic dislocation within our societies. New Zealand should be commended for the ways in which their indigenous peoples have become true partners in the social fabric of their country. Canada has a long way to go in bridging the gap between indigenous and settler communities, between the First Nations and those of European descent in particular. Steps are being made; witness the Truth and Reconciliation Commission.[7] But these are only first steps—especially given the horror of the residential schools that sought to expunge indigenous culture, language, and sensibilities through forced separation from parents. The United States is also tending to relations between Native Americans and the rest of society, but more front and center for the church in this country is the complication of race—notably but not exclusively the black-white racial divide that is virtually part of the DNA of American society given the history of slavery. The church in these countries should recognize that it can and must play

---

[6]See, for example, Nicholas Wolterstorff, *Justice: Rights and Wrongs* (Princeton, NJ: Princeton University Press, 2010), 83.

[7]See more about the Truth and Reconciliation Commission of Canada at www.trc.ca.

an active role—not as the only player, of course—in working toward social, economic, racial, and ethnic reconciliation.[8]

So while sexuality was not an incidental theme for the Old Testament prophets, it was not the question that defined what it meant to be the people of God in exile. This leads me to wonder whether questions of human sexuality should be the critical and defining boundary between the faith of the Christian church and the society at large. Might the witness of the prophets suggest that what defines the church in such a time as this is a deep commitment to social justice, works of mercy, and advocacy for those at the margins of our society? If so, it would radically change the way that we might be perceived in the society at large.

OPTION D: THE RESPONSE OF "FAITHFUL PRESENCE" REVISITED

Finally, let us consider again the fourth option: redemptive engagement through faithful presence. On the one hand, this perspective does affirm the potential of a hopeful engagement with the secular cultural and social context. Further, it sustains a long-arc vision for transformative change in our world. It would seem that here, at least, we have a response that fulfills the vision of being "in"—present—and "not of"—that is, faithful. It gives meaning to the daily lives of Christians at home, in their neighborhoods, and through their work. And it provides them with a vision to be thoroughly Christian while accepting if not actually affirming the diversity of the culture and society in which they live and work.

But three caveats need to be mentioned. The first, stressed by James K. A. Smith in his *Awaiting the King*, is that the ultimate vision of the church is not cultural transformation—that is, making the world a better place.[9] The first responsibility of the church is to be its own culture with its own liturgies and even its own meal. The church is always countercultural in some form or another, living according to a different calendar and a distinct allegiance to another Ruler. The church is a kingdom community

---

[8]See, for example, Michael O. Emerson and Christian Smith, *Divided by Faith: Evangelical Religion and the Problem of Race in America* (Oxford: Oxford University Press, 2000).

[9]James K. A. Smith, *Awaiting the King: Reforming Public Theology* (Grand Rapids, MI: Baker Academic, 2018).

with its identity in Christ and its focus on a heavenly city. Thus our citizenship is always in another place, even if we are quite present to the earthly city. Without discounting social engagement, our first calling is to foster what Newbigin called the "hermeneutic of the gospel": a living, dynamic, Christian community that lives by and under the lordship of Christ.

And second—again per Smith in *Awaiting the King*—we must be alert and not naive to the lure or power of the culture in which we are located. Culture is a battlefield; the social and cultural default of Western society has views of power and human flourishing that fly in the face of the witness of the New Testament. The ever-present danger is that we would be assimilated such that all we have done is baptize culture or been assimilated by the culture. Unwittingly, we are immersed in the daily routines and rhythms of the earthly city that is marked by sin and death. It is not neutral terrain. Thus Smith elsewhere points out the power of the mall, for example, as a subtle counterforce to the liturgies of the faith community.[10]

Third, we must not forget that one of the key signs of the life and witness of the church is that there will be a cost. Our engagement in the world will not be easy. We must sustain a vibrant theology of what it means to be a suffering church. Our faithful presence in the world will come with seasons of difficulty.

But in all of this, we are on the journey together. Thus the engagement that we each have in our social and cultural context Monday through Friday must be matched, and even more than matched, by the shared experience of the community of faith—a liturgical, catechetical, and missional community—on mission together as the hermeneutic of the gospel.

CONCLUSION

I have attempted to show in the first part of this book what it means to live in a secular age. This is our new reality, and the world in which we are called to be the church. Rowan Williams, Welsh theologian and

---

[10]James K. A. Smith, *You Are What You Love: The Spiritual Power of Habit* (Grand Rapids, MI: Brazos Press, 2016), 40-42.

former Archbishop of Canterbury, suggests that we make a distinction between what he calls *programmatic* and *procedural* secularism.[11] Programmatic secularism assumes that the secular is the only legitimate voice in the public square and that the secular perspective is value free. In contrast, procedural secularism grants space for a religious voice and perspective—one that acknowledges that secularism is itself a mindset, an ideology, and that the religious voice needs to be allowed to address the big ticket issues of our culture/society.

Williams is not suggesting that this religious voice should be privileged or that it is beyond criticism. Rather, he is insisting that a religious perspective be included as a crucial way of recognizing that the choices and priorities for a society have some kind of moral foundation:

> Procedural secularism is the acceptance of state authority of a prior and irreducible other or others; it remains secular, because as soon as it systematically privileged one group it would ally its legitimacy with the sacred and so destroy its otherness; but it can move into and out of alliance with the perspectives of faith, depending on the varying and unpredictable outcomes of honest social argument, and can collaborate without anxiety with communities of faith in the provision, for example, of education or social regeneration.[12]

Along these same lines, Thomas E. Reynolds makes a very helpful distinction between secularism and secularity. *Secularism* is an ideology that might rightly be resisted, but *secularity* is a social and cultural location that opens up a new vista for the church and a new opportunity for mission.[13] Reynolds observes:

> The good of secularity, then, unlike secularism, is that it sets religious traditions free to contribute to the composition of social space. Correlatively, such freedom entails pluralism. No one religion should own the public sphere, monopolizing discourse. Secularity is the product of and

---

[11]Rowan Williams, "Rome Lecture: 'Secularism, Faith and Freedom,'" November 23, 2006, http://rowanwilliams.archbishopofcanterbury.org/articles.php/1175/rome-lecture-secularism-faith-and-freedom.

[12]Williams, "Rome Lecture."

[13]I have on the whole followed this suggestion from Reynolds in my references to secularity versus secularism in this book.

condition for open conversation, and such conversation is fundamental for sharing space. So secularity and pluralism, far from undermining faith traditions, are the productive founts of civic engagement, empathetic broadmindedness, and mutual accountability among religious groups. They are twins that challenge us all, religious and non-religious alike, to participate productively in fashioning a third discourse of intercultural and inter-religious mutuality.[14]

If Reynolds's argument about secularity and pluralism is valid, could it be that we see secularity as actually providential? If so, as I have been suggesting in these chapters, rather than fighting secularity or viewing it as a threat, we can speak to how this soil is potentially good for the Christian faith. We can be free to stop bemoaning our fate or wringing our hands and wondering what went wrong but instead consider the new reality to which God is calling the church. In this connection, I am struck by the words of the prophet Jeremiah when he says to the people of Judah that they are to seek the peace of the city to which God had sent them. In order to do this, they needed to see that they were there by divine appointment.

Seeking the peace of our city means that we will need to do cultural and ethnographic study so that we understand our context. Rather than assuming "bad" when we think about secularism or secularity, we view this new reality in the same way that any Christian missionary would view a culture: where are the points of connection and disconnection, continuity and discontinuity between the culture and the Christian faith? Where and in what ways does the gospel challenge the culture? In what ways is it countercultural? But then also, where are there points of synergy and connection that will open up new vistas to the gospel? What are the deep longings and aspirations of those who live and work in a secular world—yearnings that can only and ultimately be fulfilled in Christ? As noted in chapter 5, the point of connection in Haizi's poetry was the longing for home. Can we read the culture looking for aspirations for transcendence, meaning, beauty, and purpose—longings that cannot

---

[14]Thomas E. Reynolds, "*Beyond* Secularism? Rethinking the 'Secular' in a Religiously Plural Context," *Toronto Journal of Theology* 25.2 (2009): 253.

ultimately be suppressed—and consider that these seeds need to be watered and witnessed to?

This means that we listen twice as much as we speak, and that we do not presume to have answers unless we have come to some clarity about the questions that are being asked. We do not presume to own the truth but, as Newbigin would insist, we merely point to it as those who are on a journey together with others who are also seeking the truth.

Further, part two of this book will make the case that if we embrace this new reality, we need to do so with a deep commitment to sustaining an alternative Christian community—a community with a distinctive identity. We need to identify the essential and critical competencies and capacities that those who give leadership to the church need to develop, including a call to restore the catechumenate, if we are going to cultivate an alternate identity for the people of God (chapters 8, 9, and 10). Further, it behooves us to ask whether we can do this alone; thus chapter 11 will speak of the priority of ecumenism in a secular age. And, finally, we need to consider the internal dispositions that need to be cultivated for leadership for the church (chapter 12).

PART 2

FORMING THE ALTERNATIVE COMMUNITY: COMPETENCIES AND DISPOSITIONS

CULTIVATING THE CAPACITY
FOR LITURGICAL LEADERSHIP

IN THIS AND THE NEXT TWO CHAPTERS, I am going to address questions of capacity—the *competencies* we need to cultivate to give leadership to the church in a secular environment. But first we need to ask what it means to be the church. When we speak of competencies, we must never lose sight of this question. We do not make the church less churchly just because we live in a secular age. To the contrary, it is more imperative than ever that we give particular attention to our ecclesiology. To speak of leadership for the church means we are going to make some assumptions about what it means to be the church.

The church will look very different in different times and places, and will perhaps have a very different form from one social location to another. William T. Cavanaugh has called the church not so much a hospital as a *field* hospital.[1] A field hospital has a feel that is very different from a major medical center in the heart of a large city, but it is still a hospital. Thus if we are going to push the boundaries of what the church might look like, we need to be very clear on what it means to be the church. It will have different forms and expressions, but it is still the church, and to be the church means to be an *alternative* community. Grace Ji-Sun Kim and Graham Hill speak of the need to establish a community that is an alternative to ideological patriotism, sexism, and racism and maintains a radical allegiance to Christ. They talk about the need to establish an alternate ecclesial culture that reflects a new

---

[1]William T. Cavanaugh, *Field Hospital: The Church's Engagement with a Wounded World* (Grand Rapids, MI: Eerdmans, 2015).

humanity in Christ.[2] In other words, we do not need a church that is nothing more than an affirmation and endorsement of the predominant culture, reinforcing cultural mores. We need a community that cuts against the grain—a community that is oriented around a vision of the ascended Lord.

This requires thoughtful, intentional practice that reflects a conviction and vision about what it means to be the church. Thus in this and the two chapters that follow I propose that we cultivate capacities for leadership for the church with this vision in mind: the church as a *liturgical, catechetical,* and *missional* community.

By *liturgical,* I mean a community that is devoted to the act of corporate worship—the gathering of the people of God that fosters a genuine engagement with the ascended Christ, in the power and grace of the Spirit. This gathering is deeply formative in that it cultivates the distinctive identity of what it means to be the people of God.

By *catechetical,* I mean that the church is a teaching-learning community—using the language of catechesis to speak of specifically *religious* instruction. Specifically, this entails teaching and learning that grounds a person and a community in the ancient faith such that catechesis is integral to Christian initiation but also that teaching and learning are part of the very fabric of their shared life, leading each Christian believer toward growth in wisdom.

By *missional,* I mean a community of faith that intentionally seeks to witness to the reign of Christ through word and deed and thereby be a means of God's redeeming grace in the world.

In a liturgical community, leadership is priestly; in the second, leaders are teachers (and preachers); and in the third, leaders empower and equip the church to be agents of grace in the world. These three are emphasized in different denominations. Anglicans, for example, typically speak of their leadership as priests. Presbyterians speak of their clergy as "teaching elders." And within my own tradition, the Christian and Missionary Alliance, we tend to think of clergy as those whose primary orientation is to empower and equip God's people for mission. In a secular

---

[2]Grace Ji-Sun Kim and Graham Hill, *Healing Our Broken Humanity: Practices for Revitalizing the Church and Renewing the World* (Downers Grove, IL: InterVarsity Press, 2018).

age, all three perspectives need to inform what it means to provide leadership for the church.

These are not mutually exclusive, of course. Below I will speak of peacekeeping and conflict mediation, and will locate this competency within the missional community. But we cannot bring a ministry of reconciliation to the world if we are not passing the peace within the church; if we are conflicted as a church community, we can hardly be instruments of conflict resolution in the world. Further, our shared liturgy only has authenticity if it is not escapist—that is, it is only authentic if there is a deep connection between our worship and our experience in the world. Worship only has integrity if our actions in the world are marked by a commitment to social and economic justice (see Isaiah 58). Our worship is only true to the call to be the church if our experience in the world informs our prayers and if our preaching, within worship, actually empowers God's people to *be* God's people in the world.

And yet, while they are not mutually exclusive, it is helpful to locate our reflections on the essential competencies for the church in a secular age within these three dimensions of the shared life of the church. Leadership for the church in a secular age needs to be leadership that fosters the capacity of the church to be a liturgical, catechetical, and missional community.

While I am considering the particular challenge of leadership for the church as it navigates secularity, I still assume a commitment to formation in the basic capacities for ministry: preaching, teaching, evangelism and initiation into Christian faith, pastoral care, and liturgical leadership. These competencies are foundational to congregational leadership in any time and culture. But, as noted above, I am suggesting that we give particular attention to the question of how to navigate secularity. This is a very complex social and cultural context, and it will require time to form leaders in it. This means that we need to resist the pressure on seminaries and programs in theological formation for church leaders to shortchange their students out of some sense of urgency. We should express concern when denominations dramatically reduce the requirements for credentialed leadership in the church. Speed is not typically a pedagogical virtue. We need to insist that our students need a full-orbed theological and pastoral formation—a full academic and intellectual process of rigorous study complemented by a comprehensive approach to both spiritual formation and supervised field experience. This has *never* been so vital for the life and ministry of the church.

And I want to appeal to those who recognize a call to credentialed ministry: do not rush the process; do not take shortcuts. Rather, tend to and cultivate the key capacities and inner dispositions that will sustain a lifetime of effective ministry engaged in the life and mission of the church. All who recognize this call need to take responsibility for their own education and formation. If we recognize a call to ministry, we need to be self-directed; we need to know what it is that we need to know and be able to do—competency—and resolve to develop that capacity, wherever and however we can get the education, training, and apprenticeship. Some of these capacities may well come through a course, workshop, or seminar; others will be learned through field experience with a good mentor. Either way, I urge emerging leaders to pay close attention to these essential capacities for leadership in the church in our day.

None of these—literally none of them—were the focus of my graduate theological study program in the 1970s. Given the changes that were afoot even then, it would have made sense for at least some of these to be part of my education. But they were not. Whatever our excuse then, there is no excuse now: these are *essential* capacities for leadership in this time and in this place.

A LITURGICAL COMMUNITY

In speaking of liturgical leadership, we must first speak of what it means to form a community that is shaped by the experience of a real-time encounter with the risen and ascended Christ. In a secular age, few things are more crucial than that we cultivate and establish a distinctive identity as a people whose primary vision and orientation is the transcendent reality of the incarnate, crucified, risen, and ascended Christ Jesus. Leadership for the church must necessarily include liturgical leadership: the *priestly* capacity to bring the people of God into the presence of Christ and, in turn, to mediate Christ to the people.

The church cannot effectively be the church in a secular context if it does not sustain a distinctive identity as the people of God. This identity is formed by a particular narrative and finds its generative strength through an encounter in worship of the risen and ascended Christ. This means that the church cannot merely be a religious club; rather, it should be a community whose contours and character is shaped by the gospel. For the church to be shaped by the gospel refers not to its ideas or theology or doctrine so much as that the people know it is the encounter with the ascended Christ in real time that defines them and their shared life.

Liturgical leadership is about cutting against the grain of what James K. A. Smith calls secular liturgies—the liturgies of the mall and other places that are deeply formative, even if unwittingly so. Both sacred and secular liturgies are all about one thing: the formation of the imagination. Or, to use more ancient language, worship orders the affections; it cultivates desire. Christian worship at its best cultivates a profound awareness of Christ and the benevolence of God—the love of God in Christ—that in turn shapes our vision of the world and life in the world.[3]

In response, the shared liturgy of the people of God needs to have four distinguishing marks that make it both intentionally Christian and intentionally formative.

- It is governed by a theological integrity, most notably that it is intentionally trinitarian and christocentric.

- It cultivates a real-time encounter with the ascended Christ that is mediated through song, word, and sacrament.

- It renews hope against the backdrop of lament.

- It engenders a rich appreciation for the power of liturgical art and space.

---

[3]Alexander Schmemann, in *For the Life of the World*, observes that secularism is not atheism or the absence of religion. It is, rather, the refusal to worship God as God. It is the negation of worship, the denial that we are worshipping beings (118). Thus he concludes: "Once we discover the true *lex orandi*, the genuine meaning and power of our *leitourgia*, once it becomes again the source of an all-embracing world view and the power of living up to it—then and only then the unique antidote to 'secularism' shall be found. And there is nothing more urgent today than this rediscovery, and this return—not to the past—but to the light and life, to the truth and grace that are eternally fulfilled by the Church when she becomes—in her *leitourgia*—that which she is" (134).

THEOLOGICAL INTEGRITY

Worship is formative only if there is a theological congruence that engages both heart and mind so that inner transformation and the vision for life and work is informed by God and the ways of God in the world. We can and must resist any notion that worship is only about sentimentality and good feelings, or even that what is happening emotionally is the prime criterion by which it is judged. Warm, positive feelings—consolations—that are not informed by a vision of God and the work of God in the world are nothing but a distraction from the deep formation of the Spirit.

This means two things. First, Christian worship is profoundly trinitarian: any outsider coming into the community of faith recognizes that this community dwells in and delights in the one who is Father, Son, and Holy Spirit. As we saw in both Ambrose and Augustine, we are only truly formed in the faith when our interior dispositions and our vision for the world are shaped by a profound awareness of the triune character of the living God.

But we also need to speak not merely of who God is but also of what God has done. We tell the story of God. All lives are shaped by some narrative, some story that gives meaning—to our lives, our relationships, and our work. Every country has a narrative (no doubt a selective one) that gives meaning to national identity. This narrative is marked out by special days, whether it is a day celebrating the founding of the nation (as in the United States) or the Queen's birthday (for members of the British Commonwealth). Christians affirm as the essential backdrop to our vision for life that God is Creator and Redeemer of all things. Thus the sequence of creation-fall-redemption is assumed in everything we say and sing. More specifically, our lives are shaped by the narrative of the birth, life, death, resurrection, and ascension of Jesus, along with the outpouring of the Spirit, all with a hopeful anticipation of the consummation of the reign of Christ.

For the church the Jesus story provides meaning, purpose, and hope. Thus there is no substitute for preaching that consistently and intentionally speaks of and arises out of the grand narrative of creation and redemption, the history of Israel, the Christ-story and the experience of the early church. We are always telling the story of God, the one who has created all things and now in Christ and by the power of the Spirit is redeeming all things.

It makes sense that preaching and the whole of worship would be located within the sequence of the historic church calendar. Calendars give meaning to our lives, be it the Roman calendar of January through December, the school calendar that is launched in September, or the fiscal calendar that marks out the tax year. All people live by a calendar that gives structure and orientation to their lives.[4] For the church, it is the Jesus story that gives meaning and infuses our shared consciousness because we tell it again and again, from Advent to Christ the King Sunday. As Bobby Gross puts it, when we live within the Christian year we come to "inhabit the story of God."[5] It should strike us as strange when a church community gives more attention to Valentine's Day and Mother's Day than it does to Pentecost. In a cultural context where some elements of the Christian calendar are being secularized—such as Christmas and Easter—the church urgently needs to affirm that *this* is the calendar, and thus *the* story, that most profoundly shapes our shared identity. And so we tell the story again and again, starting afresh each year on the first Sunday of Advent.

ENCOUNTER WITH THE ASCENDED CHRIST

Then second, Christian worship is at its heart an encounter with the transcendent "other," as the people of God enter into a different sphere of reality. No one gets this as markedly as those in the Eastern traditions who speak of how in the Eucharist we have stepped into the holy of holies. But I am suggesting that all liturgical leadership is about fostering the awareness that this event, this gathering, bridges heaven and earth. We are not just *talking* about God; we are *meeting* God in Christ through the gracious empowerment of the Spirit. We have stepped into heaven.

---

[4]I am grateful to Terry Fach, a colleague, for speaking to the reality of the diverse calendars and why the church calendar matters more than ever.

[5]Bobby Gross, *Living the Christian Year: Time to Inhabit the Story of God* (Downers Grove, IL: InterVarsity Press, 2009).

And thus, fundamentally, Christian worship cannot be narcissistic. It is not all about us; it is, rather, all about Jesus. It is the premier act by which we de-center our lives and are reminded that the world does not revolve around us or our family or our nation-state or even our problems. We intentionally move into a zone, a shared space, where we are conscious that another—Jesus, our *living hope* (1 Peter 1:3)—merits all our shared praise and adoration. In worship we are realigned; our minds are set on things above (Colossians 3:2).

This encounter with the risen and ascended Christ is mediated to us through three fundamental actions: songs and hymns of praise and prayer, the Scriptures read and proclaimed, and the Table celebrated. In each of these our attentiveness is to the Spirit, who draws us into the presence of Christ. Thus the sermon is not first and foremost an encounter with a text; the text is a means to an end—that we see Jesus and hear his voice of comfort, encouragement, and admonition. The Lord's Table is not and cannot be a mere memorial; it is a transformative encounter with Christ Jesus himself.

These remarks assume that the presence and power of the Spirit in the life of the church is anchored in two practices: the ministry of the Word and the ministry of the Table. Our songs and hymns of praise come before, during, and in response to those two events by which Christ is present to the church: the Word read and proclaimed, and the Meal celebrated. These are the universals that cross centuries and cultures; in many respects, these two actions make the church the church (see Acts 2:42).

Thus leadership for the church in a secular age will necessarily mean the restoration of the ancient art of preaching—the gracious and transformative ministry of reading and proclaiming the Scriptures. In this regard, we also need to affirm the priority of the oral reading of Scripture in addition to the faithful exposition of the text as the food and drink of the people of God.

With regard to the Table, the only hope for the church in a secular age is a recovery of the biblical and essential practice of weekly Eucharist. This too is food for the road; we form an alternative community around an alternative meal. The church is formed and sustained by the body and blood of the living and ascended Christ. Some will no doubt want to ask why this needs to be weekly. Indeed, for some evangelical Christians, anything more than quarterly or monthly will seem overly "Catholic" or sacramental. Yet it may be that a church community that truly recognizes the character of a secular age will see the need for this grace. In doing so, we follow the example of not only the ancient church, but also of the Reformers Martin Luther and John Calvin, and of John Wesley.

In other words, in a post-Christian secular age, we will get past polarizing between evangelical and sacramental and pentecostal; we will necessarily come to see—as Newbigin stressed—that the church needs to be all three.

HOPE AGAINST A BACKDROP OF LAMENT

Third, true worship sustains hope in a difficult and fragmented world. But hope is always—unequivocally always—spoken against the backdrop of lament. True worship is always an act of renewed hope; we should come from our worship with a fresh appreciation of the power and grace of God in our lives and in our world as we return to the challenges, perplexities, and complications of life. Worship must cut against the grain of despair and cynicism or any proclivity we might have toward fatalism.

Thus, as was stressed in the chapter on the wisdom from the exilic prophets, true worship cannot be one happy song after another. Rather, those who lead us in our songs and hymns and guide us through our prayers must know what it means to sing "when sorrows like sea billows roll" and bring us to a renewed confidence that "it is well with my soul." Formative worship is not escapist; rather, as we see so clearly in the Psalms, it brings the deep angst of the human condition into the prayers and songs of the worshiping community.

This means that true liturgical leadership includes leading the faith community in lament—in naming deep disappointment, pain, and loss. Without lament we only have pseudo-hope; we are left with nothing but sentimental optimism. Instead, lament is able to lead us to a renewed and sustainable hope and confidence in the risen and ascended Christ, who will do God's work in God's time.

THE POWER OF LITURGICAL ART AND SPACE

In speaking of liturgical leadership for an alternative community in a secular age, we also, fourth, need to reflect on the significance of liturgical space and liturgical art. We cannot afford to underestimate the power of space, sacred space, when it comes to the worship, learning, and witness of a faith community. We are embodied souls; spaces are not neutral but either affirm or undercut our theological convictions about God and the purposes of God in our world. As Rowan Williams put it so well in *A Silent Action*: "The decay of Christian liturgical art always goes hand in hand with the degeneration of the spiritual life. . . . The refusal to bring one's full creative capacities to the service of God is a betrayal of the whole Christian calling to 'reintegration' of the world." He quotes Thomas Merton as calling this "a rank infidelity to God the Creator and to the Sanctifying Spirit of Truth."[6] Tomáš Halík, writing as a Christian theologian and spiritual writer out of the profound secularity of the Czech Republic, puts it this way: "I have found that few things prove as reliable an indicator of the health, depth, and authenticity of some community's spirituality as its sensitivity—or lack of it—to beauty, one of the traditional characteristics of God."[7]

Thus our liturgical spaces and music must be marked not by banality and sentimentality but by the depth and breadth of the very best creative and imaginative genius our community and our society has to offer to the giver of all good gifts. This is not necessarily limited to high liturgical art. The art that shapes our shared worship needs to include the common crafts of our quilt makers, our weavers, and the skilled carpenters and gardeners who tend to the landscapes around our worship spaces. Within

---

[6]Rowan Williams, *A Silent Action: Engagements with Thomas Merton* (Louisville, KY: Fons Vitae, 2011), 36. Williams then quotes Merton again from his book *Disputed Questions*: "To *like* bad sacred art, and to feel that one is *helped* by it in prayer, can be a symptom of real spiritual disorders." No doubt this will strike some as an overstatement. After all, does not anything that helps us in the spiritual life have some value? But perhaps we think this because we still do not appreciate how significant art is to the life of the church. David Taylor challenges us on this score, insisting that we must pursue excellence. Bad art is anything that is "cliché, melodramatic, cheap, rushed, plastic, superficialized, elitist, garish, lazy, cold, self-indulgent, and impersonal." See W. David O. Taylor, *For the Beauty of the Church: Casting a Vision for the Arts* (Grand Rapids, MI: Baker Books, 2010), 150.

[7]Tomáš Halík, *Night of the Confessor: Christian Faith in an Age of Uncertainty*, trans. Gerald Turner (New York: Image Books, 2012), 54.

our communities of faith there are actors, dancers, and singers who can bring remarkable grace and talent to Christ as a contribution to our shared sacrifice of praise. We can embrace the joy and deep consolation that comes with Gregorian chant, with its enduring power over centuries, and also the grace of jazz vespers. We can delight in the power of stained glass that infuses our shared space with light and grace as well as in the exquisite work of one of the quilt makers in the congregation.

Artists in our midst—the poets, musicians, graphic designers, and painters—speak to and give voice to the deep yearnings of our culture that in the end will find fulfillment in Christ. Further, the artists in our midst are essential to our capacity to lament and restore hope. This is the way of the Old Testament prophets like Ezekiel: we use words, yes, but words as often as not in the form of poetry, which is in turn accompanied by powerful images and dramatic representations.

CONCLUSION

Beyond these four markers of transformative worship in a post-Christian and secular age, consider also the following practical suggestions. First, we need to get past the idea that worship leaders are one and the same as local musicians. Liturgical leadership is a calling and responsibility of all of those who are called into leadership in the life and witness of the church. Musicians will play a key role, no doubt, but we must not equate musical capacity with leadership in worship.

Second, we need to realize that this priestly side of leadership—liturgical leadership—is a learned art. The competencies of liturgical leadership must be cultivated, and mastered as an essential part of providing leadership for the church in a secular age.

Third, we need to emphasize liturgical *hospitality*. In the next chapter, I will be speaking of the need to cultivate a teaching-learning community and, in particular, of what it means to be more intentionally catechetical for those who are on a journey to Jesus. It needs to be stressed that the journey to Jesus, in a post-Christian, secular context, could be an extended journey. It might actually take a number of years. This means that those who are on the journey to faith might well be part of the church community for some time before they come to faith in Christ. They will belong in order to believe.[8]

If this is the case, it follows that the liturgical life of the church must be marked by an intentional hospitality. This does not necessarily mean that we need to cater to or focus on the inquirer. Worship for the Christian community can be unapologetically distinct and other-centered, with a focus on the ascended Christ. For secular people, this will be a strange experience, and understandably so. But, over time, as they belong to and experience the love of the Christian community, they will come to a growing appreciation of the love of God *in Christ*.

The genius of such a community is that this person can be present as we let the Spirit do the Spirit's work in the Spirit's time. We do not rush the process or try to choreograph the journey. Those who are inquirers will be part of the liturgy of the Christian community. Without apologizing that it is other-centered or strange, we will not merely allow but encourage them to come alongside. We will trust that God will meet them over time, that the love of Christ will be present to them, and that the Spirit will draw them into the truth.

Does this mean that the church in a post-Christian and secular age should come to see the Lord's Table as a means by which the hospitality of Christ is revealed to those who are on a journey to Jesus? Might we consider, in other words, an *open* table where all are welcome, including those who are on the way to faith? However we answer that particular question, we must welcome those who are inquirers to our worship— and our worship, distinct and other, will in itself be a powerful testimony to the living presence of Christ.

Ultimately, conversion is not about believing certain things to be true, but about meeting the ascended Christ in real time. This is the very purpose of the church's liturgical practice: to cultivate a deep appreciation that Christ is on the throne of the universe.

---

[8]Elsewhere I have made the case, as many others have, that in a secular age conversion will be more of a journey than an event, and that this has significant implications for the way in which the church is present to those who are on this journey. See Gordon T. Smith, *Beginning Well: Christian Conversion and Authentic Transformation* (Downers Grove, IL: InterVarsity Press, 2001); and Gordon T. Smith, *Transforming Conversion: Re-Thinking the Language and Contours of Christian Initiation* (Grand Rapids, MI: Baker Academic, 2010).

9

CULTIVATING THE CAPACITY
FOR CATECHETICAL LEADERSHIP

THE CHURCH IS A TEACHING-LEARNING COMMUNITY. Disciples are made by baptism and teaching (Matthew 28:20), and the early church devoted themselves to the teaching of the apostles (Acts 2:42). While this has always been true, there is a particular need for it in this time and in this place. The church can thrive in a secular world only if the Christian community is nothing less than a school of lifelong learning toward wisdom in Christ. The level of immaturity in the church is astonishing; this is due, in part, to the juvenilization of the liturgy, but also to a lack of teaching. Craig Dykstra is convinced that there is a powerful hunger in Christian churches that can only be met through a reincorporation of the intentional spiritual practice of theological education for the whole people of God—old and young, new Christian and older Christian.[1] The goal, of course, is that we might grow up in the faith, maturing in Christ who is our living head (Ephesians 4:15). This clearly was a defining priority for the apostle Paul, who spoke of his vigorous commitment—all the energy within him—to teach everyone with all wisdom to present each one mature in Christ (Colossians 1:28-29).

The church is then a worshiping community that is also a school: narrating the Christian story, hearing the Scriptures, and interpreting them in a way that allows them to infuse heart and mind and inform our lives, our work, and our relationships in the world. It is a lifelong journey of growing in wisdom, always attentive to new insights, new perspectives, new ways of engaging the ancient faith for the new challenges we are

---

[1]Craig Dykstra, *Growing in the Life of Faith: Education and Christian Practices*, 2nd ed. (Louisville, KY: Westminster John Knox, 2005).

facing. And as we get older, we turn to pass on the faith to the generation that follows. We are mentors, guides, conversation partners, all within a vibrant community of teaching and learning. To grow older and not wiser is a tragedy; indeed, all who are older, the Scriptures suggest, should be capable of teaching (Hebrews 5:12).

Those who are leaders must model this and make it a priority. Leadership assumes the capacity to teach and the commitment to teaching—to teach others who then in turn are also capable of teaching (2 Timothy 2:2). Teaching is happening on many fronts, of course—as a key part of a youth gathering, a men's breakfast, an early-morning women's professional group, or a morning coffee for retired men and women. All of this is an essential complement to shared worship. Why not also insist on an adult Bible study class that comes week in and week out before or after corporate worship? Why not make a regular study of the ancient creeds something that is ongoing in the life of the church so that when we say the words, "I believe," we know of what we speak? We must commit to growing in a faith that is deeply formed by thoughtful engagement with the God who has been revealed as triune.

RESTORING THE ANCIENT CATECHUMENATE

While this commitment to be a school of wisdom is reflected in an ongoing call to the whole congregation, this vision will only be part of the DNA of a church if its leaders make teaching and learning integral to the very process of coming to faith in Christ. That is, we need to give particular attention to catechesis and to a restoration of the ancient catechumenate.

The Scriptures and the creedal confession shape the church's shared identity. And few things feed this identity as much as the commitment to study and learning and teaching as part of Christian *initiation*. Evangelism needs to be located within the life of the church as a teaching-learning community. Part of restoring the ancient catechumenate means reintegrating evangelism and catechesis.

I use the language of "catechesis" intentionally. Some may wonder why I am not speaking of "discipleship" or "spiritual formation." Why use the less-than-familiar language of catechesis, which might seem more appropriate for a uniquely Catholic, Anglican, or Orthodox readership? The reason for this language is twofold.

First, discipleship is the commitment to formation that includes worship, teaching, learning, equipping for, and being formed in active service in the world. In other words, the whole of what it means to be a liturgical, catechetical, and missional community is discipleship. Worship is discipleship; mission is discipleship; and teaching is discipleship. But catechesis is a very particular thing: it is religious instruction, a teaching and learning that cultivates knowledge and wisdom in the faith. Discipleship includes but is not restricted to teaching.

Second, the language of catechesis takes us back to the wisdom of the early church so we can see the parallels to our own pluralist and secular social environment. If coming to faith—conversion—is more a process than an event, if becoming a Christian is a journey, then surely we need to see that evangelism and teaching are integrated, and indeed we need to reflect on the continuing value of the ancient catechumenate. In the ancient church, as Simon Chan has stated so well, "the catechumenate became a means of conversion rather than of nurturing converts," and now we are learning that "the key to making a real Christian is still the catechumenate."[2] Walter Brueggemann speaks to something similar when he says that the "task of prophetic ministry is to nurture, nourish, and evoke a consciousness and perception alternative to the consciousness and perception of the dominant culture around us."[3] In other words, the ancient catechumenate is designed to cultivate an alternate vision and way of being. Without something rigorous like this, the person coming to faith remains essentially secular in outlook and disposition.

As noted in chapter 4, one of the major contributions of the pre-Christendom church to our own era is its wisdom around the practices of Christian initiation. We urgently need to cultivate distinctive identity and what Gerald Sittser calls a "functional maturity."[4] The very process of coming to faith includes not merely incorporation into Christian

---

[2]Simon Chan, *Liturgical Theology: The Church as a Worshipping Community* (Downers Grove, IL: IVP Academic, 2006), 105.

[3]Walter Brueggemann, *The Prophetic Imagination* (Minneapolis: Fortress, 1978), 13.

[4]Gerald Sittser, "The Catechumenate and the Rise of Christianity," *Journal of Spiritual Formation and Soul Care* 6.2 (November 2013): 202.

community but also the cultivation of the capacities for spiritual growth. That is, the journey to faith by which a person is brought into Christian community consists of not merely a "decision" for Jesus but a rigorous process by which new Christians now have within them the habits of heart and mind, the disciplines of daily routines, by which they will grow in the grace of God. They will not remain perpetually infants in Christ.

One contemporary example of how the ancient catechumenate is being adapted for a contemporary context is the Catholic Rite for the Christian Initiation of Adults (RCIA) instituted as a direct consequence of Vatican II.[5] In some parishes, the RCIA is ongoing, but some invite those who are interested to join a weekly conversation and study group in the later part of the church calendar, an initial step in a three-phase process:

- A time of inquiry—where questions are asked and clarifications offered—typically through the months of September, October, and November leading to Advent

- A time of instruction—with a focus on the creeds—from the beginning of Advent until the last Sunday prior to Ash Wednesday

- A time of preparation for baptism during the season of Lent, leading up to the baptism itself at the Easter vigil on the Saturday evening of Holy Week

At each stage, the individual is invited to confirm if they wish to move ahead with the process—the first Sunday of Advent to become a catechumen, and then the first Sunday of Lent to accept the declaration that they are indeed of the "elect."

When it comes to evangelism, rather than speaking of decisions for Jesus it is imperative that we change our language and speak of a journey to Jesus. Those who are coming to the faith from a secular background need a full orientation and immersion in this new culture, this new language, this new way of being as they move toward baptism. Thus, why

---

[5]*Rite of Christian Initiation of Adults*, United States ed. (Washington, DC: United States Catholic Conference, 1988); *Rite of Christian Initiation of Adults*, Canadian ed. (Ottawa: Publications Service of the Canadian Conference of Catholic Bishops, 1987). See also Thomas H. Morris, *The RCIA: Transforming the Church: A Resource for Pastoral Implementation* (Mahwah, NJ: Paulist Press, 1989).

not be intentional? Perhaps each September we make an announcement during morning worship that there will be a weekly gathering for those who might like to explore the claims of Jesus and the way of Jesus. Perhaps we put it this way:

> If you would like to enter into this journey toward faith in Christ—if you would like to test the waters and see if this is where the Spirit is leading you—then join our weekly conversation between now and Easter. We will use as our curriculum a focused study of the New Testament letter of 1 Peter. Along the way, you will get a full orientation to the whole of the biblical narrative and the Jesus story, and we will help you to learn what it means to live in genuine Christian community.
>
> It is a nine-month process. After a season of exploration between now and the first Sunday of Advent, we will continue to explore the faith and move intentionally toward not merely understanding but a heartfelt encounter with Christ. When we come to the season of Lent, you will have a chance to answer the question: Are you in? If you go all the way to Easter, you will be baptized into the faith and into Christian community.

In other words, do not ask people to come to faith in Christ when they have yet to consider what it truly means and count the cost. Let them join the Christian community to see and feel how the Scriptures shape the life of the community of faith, to see how together we are learning how to love one another, and, most of all, to get to know this Jesus who at the end of the process will be asking them himself: "Will you follow me?"

The church can make no assumptions about the intellectual, emotional, or moral life of a person coming to faith in Christ. Thus a process is needed to nurture them in the faith, a process that leads not merely to baptism but toward a functional maturity—or, at the very least, constitutes a good beginning that increases the possibility that they will have a distinctive identity as a Christian believer who is able to be in but not of the world, is a contributing member of the Christian community, and is growing in faith, hope, and love.

This is a critical agenda for a Christian community. The grave danger is that we would vaccinate people against genuine Christianity—that they would "come" to faith but not actually "get" the faith so that it is in their bones, that they would not become functionally mature in their faith. It is essential that they experience a coming to faith that is not a mere pinprick but a thorough baptism into a new form of existence—one in which, while they start out as infants, they have a foundation of intellectual, emotional, and ethical dispositions in place that will assure growth to maturity in Christ.

1 PETER AS A RESOURCE FOR CATECHESIS

As we saw above in the sample announcement, one possibility is that we would use 1 Peter as our guide to Christian initiation and catechesis—particularly given how this New Testament letter seems to uniquely focus on what it means to be Christian as a minority presence. Peter speaks explicitly to the need for Christians to be established in our faith in 5:9, but it is his theme throughout. And as I noted in chapter 3, the letter is intended as both guidance and encouragement regarding how to live as a minority religious presence in a pagan or pluralist world. Clearly the journey to maturity in Christ in this context includes intellect and understanding, the ordering of the affections and the strengthening of volition, the will.

This would suggest that, in using 1 Peter as a resource for catechesis, first we need to consider the matter of identity. Christian initiation and catechesis—the essential groundwork by which we are formed in the faith—finds its orientation around our intellectual, emotional, social, and thus spiritual location. Peter is quite eloquent on this point, saying that the church is the company of those who through mercy have been brought into a living hope in the risen Christ Jesus; we have an inheritance in him and are, in him, protected by the power of God (1 Peter 1:3-12). This is for us a deep joy—"an indescribable and glorious joy" (1 Peter 1:8)—for, even though we do not see Christ as yet face to face, we love him and we are confident that in him we will know the salvation of God.

Even though the letter speaks of the people of God as aliens and exiles (1 Peter 2:11), that does not mean we have no identity. Rather, we are being built into a spiritual house with Christ as the chief cornerstone and now, in Christ, the church is a "a chosen race, a royal priesthood, a holy nation, God's own people" (1 Peter 2:9).

The letter is marked by a clear and thorough focus on who Christ is. It is the Christ story that gives us both the theological and literary structure of the letter. Peter opens with a reference to the resurrection, and later makes a reference to the ascension and a deep assurance of the ultimate revelation and triumph of Christ. But running throughout the letter is the theme of the suffering and death of Christ: "You know that you were ransomed from the futile ways inherited from your ancestors, not with perishable things like silver or gold, but with the precious blood of Christ, like that of a lamb without defect or blemish" (1 Peter 1:18).

It is through this Christ (1 Peter 1:21) that the church has come to faith and has a hope that is set on God. It is through this Christ that the church is being built into a spiritual house. Then, further, we read:

> He himself bore our sins in his body on the cross, so that, free from sins, we might live for righteousness; by his wounds you have been healed. (1 Peter 2:24)

> For Christ also suffered for sins once for all, the righteous for the unrighteous, in order to bring you to God. He was put to death in the flesh, but made alive in the spirit, in which also he went and made a proclamation to the spirits in prison. (1 Peter 3:18-19)

The suffering of Christ helps us make sense of our own suffering, reminding us, in the words of Paul in Romans 8:17, that we are joint heirs with Christ in his suffering. Peter puts it this way: "But rejoice insofar as you are sharing Christ's sufferings, so that you may also be glad and shout for joy when his glory is revealed" (1 Peter 4:13).

So what does this mean for catechesis? It means, quite simply, that a person coming to faith is present for and attentive to the drumbeat of the Jesus story week in and week out. We need to tell the Jesus story again and again so that it is in our bones and defines us like nothing else. And it is into this Christ that we are baptized (1 Peter 3:18-22); through baptism we are drawn into a relationship of devotion and allegiance. Baptism represents or symbolizes our identity.

Thus we need to affirm again the value of the Christian calendar for the liturgical life of the church. What the calendar does is reinforce that the Jesus story is our story, so that the narrative of the birth, life, death, and resurrection of Christ defines us. This is our intellectual vision for catechesis: to foster this mind, this vision for life and work and relationships, this way of seeing.

TWO CRUCIAL CAPACITIES/PRACTICES

As we are found "in Christ," there are two essential resources without which we cannot hope to sustain our identity: the Scriptures and the Christian community. These are the indispensable ways and means by which the Christian is sustained in the faith.

The Scriptures. In speaking about his readers' identity in Christ, Peter observes that they were born anew by the living and enduring Word of God (1 Peter 1:23). He speaks of the life-giving and eternal quality of this Word that was proclaimed to them (1 Peter 1:25). Then he urges them—like infants—to "long for the pure, spiritual milk, so that by it [they] may grow into salvation" (1 Peter 2:2). If we are going to be mature in our faith—steadfast in Christ, able to withstand the forces and pressures that would compromise our faith—it will be as we are thoroughly and completely women and men of the Word. It is through the Scriptures that, if we prepare our minds and discipline ourselves (in the words of 1 Peter 1:13), we grow and mature as we have minds that are informed and transformed by the truth.

Note that the language of 1 Peter 2:2 suggests that what is transformative is not knowledge per se but the Word as spiritual food that cultivates wisdom. It seems to echo the language of Colossians 3:16 ("let the word of Christ dwell in you richly") and the language of John 15:7 ("if . . . my words abide in you"). Thus catechesis must necessarily include immersion in, knowledge of, and attention to what it means to live by, under, and in the Scriptures. This initial immersion in the Scriptures then shapes the whole of the journey of faith; to be a growing and maturing Christian is to be a person who lives and breathes the text of Scripture.

Christian community. The fellowship of the Spirit—the church—is a recurring theme in 1 Peter. It is telling that, in a letter that speaks to how we live as a minority presence in a hostile environment, the apostle would highlight the importance of Christian community. We cannot live the Christian life in isolation from the community of faith. We need one another; we need to be in fellowship with one another.

Two aspects of our common life are highlighted in 1 Peter. First, we are called to love one another. Thus we read: "Have genuine mutual love, love one another deeply from the heart" (1 Peter 1:22); and, "All of you, have unity of spirit, sympathy, love for one another, a tender heart, and a humble mind" (1 Peter 3:8). Then later in the epistle we read: "Above all, maintain constant love for one another" (1 Peter 4:8), and Peter calls for two expressions of love: hospitality ("be hospitable to one another," 1 Peter 4:9) and service ("serve one another," 1 Peter 4:10).

Few things are so crucial to our capacity to be Christian in a secular context as that we learn how to love one another—and that we live in dynamic fellowship, in community, in a fellowship marked by our mutual love for one another expressed in hospitality and service. Douglas Harink speaks of hospitality as "open hearts, open homes, and open hands," and notes that this way of being is only possible if we do not live in fear.[6]

Second, Christian community is specifically an *authoritative* community. In 1 Peter 5:1-5, Peter speaks to those who are elders. They are urged to lead, to give oversight to the faith community—not to "lord it over" the flock, but to exercise humble, generous service, leading by example. Those who are younger are urged, in turn, to defer to the authority of those who are older. This recognizes, if not assumes, that there is some kind of structure to our common life. The community takes a form that includes the exercise of authority, deference to authority, and genuine and pastoral leadership. There is a structure to Christian community. Both the elders and those within the congregation are called to humility—humble service and deference to authority. God has no patience with the proud. In this we are reminded that Christian community is not merely a matter of being nice and generous toward one another. It is that, but it is much more than that; it is also an *authoritative* community. There is leadership; there is a board of elders; there is pastoral authority—not, again, the kind of authority that lords it over but the leadership of generous service.

---

[6]Douglas Harink, *1 & 2 Peter*, Brazos Theological Commentary on the Bible (Grand Rapids, MI: Brazos Press, 2009), 113.

How do we speak of an authoritative community when an emerging generation of Christians and Christian leaders has only seen the abuse of power and authority—leadership that is neither accountable nor transparent? If they have never experienced a truly benevolent, wise, and humble leadership, they will understandably recoil at the thought that they are supposed to come "under" any kind of authority. Surely, we can only lead such people if leadership is never an end but a means to an end—to know, love, and serve Christ. There also must be accountability and transparency in our approach to leadership. Those in leadership should listen twice as much as they speak, should lead from a disposition of faith, not fear, and should have a commitment to generosity through service. But the point remains that the church that flourishes will have some structure to it. We are not independent nomads.

THE CENTRALITY OF CHRIST

If, as we have learned from 1 Peter, there are two essential means by which we sustain our identity in Christ—the Scriptures and the church—which is most crucial? Those of the Protestant and evangelical persuasion insist that we sustain our relationship with Christ through the Word. For those with Orthodox, Catholic, or Anglo-Catholic heritage, it is supremely the church that is the means by which we are in fellowship with Christ. Which is it?

Perhaps the answer is "both/and." Indeed, it is not so much both but both *together*; the Word is received in community. We are a fellowship of the Word. Thus catechesis and Christian initiation need to include both an orientation toward the Scriptures, so that a new Christian increasingly becomes a person of this sacred text, and an incorporation into a community of faith that is learning as an authoritative community to live in mutual love (1 Peter 2:2).

Yet in the end, the bottom line is always Christ. We affirm the authority of Scripture and what it means to live within an authoritative community only with a vision ever before us of the crucified, risen, and ascended Christ. Neither the church nor the Scriptures is an end in itself; each is only a means by which we find and nurture our shared identity in Christ. Both can be deadly when no longer linked to Christ, who is revealed through the Scriptures and who is known through the life and witness of the church. Thus all true catechesis and all life-giving engagement with the Scriptures is anchored in the liturgy—the shared worship of the people of God who come into the presence of the living and ascended Christ.

This is why, as noted, 1 Peter might be the ideal text for catechesis, for it seems to have that particular agenda in mind: cultivating the capacity of young Christians to live with integrity as a minority presence, whether that be in a pagan context or, for Christians today, in a secular context. The letter speaks of identity in Christ. It speaks of an alternative way of being. It speaks of both Word and community. It speaks of suffering, which is actually a defining theme of the epistle. And it concludes with a call to both hospitality, on the one hand, and a confidence in the purposes of God on the other. Thus we are called to "stand fast" in the grace of God (1 Peter 5:12b) and not to live in fear ("do not fear what they fear," 1 Peter 3:14), with the result that we "cast all [our] anxiety on him, because he cares for [us]" (1 Peter 5:6-7).

CONCLUSION

While this chapter has stressed the importance of beginning with catechesis, teaching and learning must be integral to all the life and rhythms of the church. Children should be learning the faith. Study and learning and reflection should be key elements of what it means to be part of a church youth group. There should be multiple places and opportunities for teaching and learning so that a newly initiated Christian can be given a menu of ongoing opportunities that may be age specific or gender specific but most of which should provide opportunities for old and young to be learning together. When someone joins a faith community they should be struck by this. Yes, we should be keen on worship, and (as will be stressed in the next chapter on mission) keen to make a difference in the world. But to an outside observer, a church should seem almost like a school. Actually, it *is* a school in which one and all, old and young, are immersed in the rhythms and routines of study, learning, debate, and reflection, growing together in knowledge and wisdom.

10

CULTIVATING THE CAPACITY
FOR MISSIONAL LEADERSHIP

IN ADDITION TO PROVIDING BOTH LITURGICAL and catechetical leadership, leaders for the church in a secular age are called to cultivate the capacity of the church to be missionally engaged, making a difference for God in witness to the reign of Christ in the world. The church in a post-Christian and secular society is not in retreat mode; the community of faith is called to be salt and light in the social and cultural location in which it has been placed—to seek redemptive engagement. Missional leadership is about the capacity to equip God's people to be on mission with Christ and the Spirit in their world. It is helpful to recognize that this engagement—equipping the church to be in the world—requires a particular set of competencies, and three in particular:

- preaching for Monday morning;
- political presence and civic engagement; and
- peacemaking and conflict resolution.

The mission of the church will include more, but these three are foundational. In a sense, they serve as a precursor to any other form of witness and missional encounter. Or, putting it differently, these three practices set the stage for all the ways in which the church fulfills its mission in the world.

PREACHING FOR MONDAY MORNING

The worship of God's people, typically on a Sunday, will without doubt be marked by the intentional proclamation of the Scriptures, the continual reference to the story of God as Creator and Redeemer, and emphasis on the sequence of the Christ events that frame everything that we do: his incarnation, life, death, resurrection, ascension, gift of the Spirit, and ultimate triumph. All, of course, is seen through the lens of the triune character of God and thus of the faith.

However, we also preach with the realization that we are not merely the people of God who have gathered. Yes, we have gathered, but we have come together as a people who are very much in the world. We gather as those who on Monday morning will be in the schools, businesses, art galleries, and legislative assemblies of our society. Can we preach in such a way that we sustain a vivid connection to the world and equip women and men to be agents of peace in that world (as they, in the language of Jeremiah 29:7, "seek the welfare of the city")? Yes, of course, we preach the whole counsel of God. But I am suggesting here that we preach in light of where hearers will be from Monday to Friday and with a view to empowering them to be actively engaged within their social and cultural contexts.

When I was a seminary student, the entire focus of the curriculum in pastoral theology was on church growth. The sign that we were effective as pastors and preachers was that our church was larger week by week by week. We emphasized the need for attractive approaches to both worship and preaching that led to larger congregations in larger facilities, even if this meant that other churches nearby were getting smaller as their members chose to join our more attractive approach to congregational life.

But what if the genius of the church is not its size when the church gathers on Sunday but its social and cultural impact when the church is dispersed on Monday? What if the test of our faith is not how active we are in the church but how Christian we are in our engagement in the world the rest of the week? We need the church to be a growing and flourishing community; no one debates that. I am merely suggesting that our orientation is not toward growth per se. Should not our preaching and teaching be about empowering women and men to be what they are called to be in the world? We preach, in other words, in such a way that, regardless of the text of the day, the orientation is toward the world in which people are called to live and work with a kingdom vision Monday through Friday. If, per Lesslie Newbigin's observation, the congregation as a whole is a hermeneutic of the gospel, then come Monday this hermeneutic is lived out in the world. We are not merely the church gathered; we are also the church dispersed and present in the world.

One potential way to move our preaching in this direction is to imagine three particular groups, each of which plays an influential role in society: those called into business, education, and the arts. These women and men have leverage: those in business, including both employees and those who own their own businesses; those in education, both in public schools and in universities and colleges; and those in music, theater, dance, media, architecture, and sculpture. Without doubt, there are many more present on Sunday morning who may not fit any of these groupings. I suggest these three not as exclusive representatives of what it means to be in the world but as those who are uniquely positioned to be a redemptive presence in the world because of the depth and breadth of their impact within a society.

Those in business touch all of us. We are all impacted by those who are called into the production of goods and services. All of us each week are buying, selling, or living with the services and products that we have purchased. Every day of our lives is in some form or another shaped by those whose shape the economy.

Those in education have perhaps more leverage than anyone to shape the hearts and minds of a people. Leaders are formed through education. Teachers know that they have this potential and this influence, particularly through the formative years when a person is an undergraduate in a university.

And then, third, those in the arts are at another inflection point in society. Our deep sensibilities are informed by the spaces where we live and work and worship—reflecting the impact of architects and designers. Musicians, dancers, and poets likewise have extraordinary capacity to impact the emotional contours of our lives.

Pastors have everything to gain by getting to know these people—visiting their offices, studios, and schools so that you can imagine them in their places of work even as you prepare to proclaim the Word. Consider where they will be, who they will be with, and the challenges they will be facing on Monday morning. Read business journals and art magazines, and keep up with current affairs in the field of education—primary, secondary, and higher education. We only preach for Monday morning when we have some level of understanding or appreciation of what our audience does. And we shouldn't just preach for and to artists; we should learn to tend to the arts in the cultivation of our own imaginations as preachers and leaders. We should allow artists—poets, musicians, designers, architects, actors, and sculptors—to be teachers and prophets in our churches. We should also be aware that those whose work is the classroom are in a powerful location within a society to shape the mind and form the hearts and imaginations of those who will shape and influence our societies tomorrow.

The point is that the reign of Christ comes not so much on Sunday morning, when the people of God gather, as on Monday morning when they are dispersed to the offices, art studios, and schools and universities where they spend the bulk of their time. The real difference a congregation makes is not determined by its size but by whether the people of God are equipped and empowered to be salt and light in their world.

Preach, then, not to attract more people to your church; preach, rather, with a vision for what it means to be the people of God in the world. Anchor what Christians do in the world in a vision of the reign of Christ—the story of God's work as Creator and Redeemer and the deep confidence we have that good will triumph over evil. Preach in such a way that they can see and feel how their work matters and how their small actions can have ripple effects in their workplaces. Assure them of the presence of the Spirit who goes before them, guides their steps, comforts them through times of discouragement, and gives them the words to say when they need to speak and the strength of heart and mind to be calm and not be caught up in a culture of fear. Preach in a way that fosters their capacity to view the workplace as a source of grace, not merely as a point of stress. Preach not to a mindset that thinks "thank God it's Friday," but rather to those who are deeply engaged, seeing challenges and opportunities through the lens of the grace of God in the world. Seek to equip them to be attentive to how the Spirit is at work in the world and to show them how to sustain spiritual practices that are distinctly about fostering their capacity to be in and thrive in the workplace.

Yes, there will be those "thank God it's Friday" weeks. That is a reminder that we must preach hope; we need to know how to encourage. Surely part of the ministry of preaching is sustaining hope in a difficult and fragmented world—preaching that acknowledges that the world is, indeed, challenging, filled with points of disappointment, difficult working relationships, and a tenuous economy. With no sentimentality or pseudo-optimism, we must learn to speak a word in season such that, regardless of the text or the theme of the sermon, both the tone and the content of our communication leans into the assurance that God is good and God is present to our world.

POLITICAL PRESENCE AND CIVIC ENGAGEMENT

When I was a seminary student in the 1970s, politics was viewed as inherently suspect. We knew that there was a political science department as an option for undergrad studies, but those of us who studied for ministry seemed to be living in a completely different universe. We were not taught the elements of what it means to be political. We did not view it as essential or integral to what it meant to provide leadership for the church.

This kind of thinking is no longer an option. Effective leadership for the church in a secular age necessarily means that we cultivate the capacity to think and act with an attentiveness to the *political*, and that means also local and global economics.

We saw in the first part of this book the need for political engagement. In the Old Testament, Esther and Daniel engaged the public square with a high level of political shrewdness. Ambrose of Milan engaged politically, sometimes in great tension, with emperors. And whether we are reading sources from historic minority churches or voices from Western Europe—notably Ellul and Bonhoeffer—we see again and again the need to learn what it means to have political wisdom.

It is helpful to think in terms of three aspects of political wisdom: the significance of presence, the importance of principled compromise, and the capacity to speak truth to power. First, consider the significance of *presence*. So much of the work of religious leaders is just a matter of showing up. We are present with no agenda other than to be there. This is work that chaplains know well; often they know that all they have done is offer the ministry of being there. Now we are all learning from chaplains that we do not always need to be useful and that being present—like a parent at a daughter's hockey game—is in itself ministry. We have no script or agenda but to show up, non-judgmentally, as friend, as chaplain, as pastor. Our presence is a *priestly* presence—we are there as pray-ers, interceding for the one and sometimes the many. We are not just getting things done, completing a to-do list. We are attentive, listening, and praying. Yes, there is more to missional engagement with our world and to what it means to be truly political. But it begins *here*. Our basis for speaking and acting is that we have been and are present.

Second, we must speak of *principled compromise*. When, in American politics, one party controls both houses of Congress and the White House, you can perhaps be a purist. When there is a majority government in the British or Canadian Parliament, they can pass legislation with little if any compromise. But otherwise, things only get done because we have learned to be bipartisan and to compromise. With the church now a minority presence, anything significant in the political sphere will come by our being able to work toward a common end with others with whom we have religious and ideological differences. We can learn to work with others toward productive outcomes; we can make common cause with those with whom we differ on ultimate questions. The one with whom we differ on ultimate matters is not the enemy; we do not need to demonize the other. Indeed, as noted in chapter 7, we need to always be contending for pluralism with tolerance, humility, and patience. This means that we are more than willing to work with those of other political persuasions and other faiths—be they Muslim or secular or agnostic—if together we can achieve a worthwhile end as we seek the common good.

Third, political wisdom also includes the ability and willingness to *speak truth to power*. Here there are two considerations. On the one hand, we need to be aware of how the political system works and of what the issues are when it comes to justice and reconciliation—to understand the issues that are impacted by our lives and our preaching. We need to learn when to speak and when to be quiet. It is often the case that less is more. If we are in a constant mode of complaint against or judgment of the local or national leadership, we can lose credibility quickly.

On the other hand, and even more crucially, we must maintain independence. We never want to lose our capacity to confront and challenge political and civil authorities. The danger is always there that we would be so aligned with one political party that we lose the capacity or the right to challenge what is clearly wrong.

Here is where the example of Billy Graham is so pertinent. In 1952, Graham got permission to hold a religious meeting on the steps of the Capitol in Washington, DC. There he announced that Christians would vote en masse in the election that fall. He publicly endorsed Dwight Eisenhower, a Republican, and openly criticized his opponent, Harry Truman. For the next twenty-plus years, Graham was often present at the White House, conducting Bible studies, praying with presidents, and linking the gospel with American destiny. It all seemed rather innocuous until it came to Richard Nixon. Graham endorsed Nixon in 1960 while attacking the other candidate, John F. Kennedy. He again endorsed Nixon in 1968, and when Nixon won Graham came to view himself as a spiritual *and* political advisor to the president. Even after the Watergate scandal broke, Graham continued to support Nixon. But then, very publicly, Graham came to see that he had so aligned himself with Nixon and that he had no voice in the Watergate affair. Graham resolved to never get enmeshed in politics again—or, better, to never grasp for political power. He was intentionally not associated with the Religious Right in the 1980s, and I cannot help but wonder what he would make of his son Franklin's vocal support of Donald Trump in the 2016 election.[1]

Ambrose of Milan is also an exemplar in this regard. He made mistakes, no doubt, but he maintained his independence. He always insisted that he was above or at least to the side of the political sphere, and always insisted on his right to confront the authorities when confrontation was called for.

---

[1]See Laurie Goodstein, "Billy Graham Warned Against Embracing a President. His Son Has Gone Another Way," *New York Times*, February 26, 2018, www.nytimes.com/2018/02/26/us /billy-graham-franklin-graham-trump.html.

When discerning whether to speak up, our timing, tone, and disposition matter. In 1 Peter we are rightly called to have an answer for the hope that is within us, but also to answer with gentleness (1 Peter 3:15-16). Note here also the words of Paul: "Conduct yourselves wisely toward outsiders, making the most of the time. Let your speech always be gracious, seasoned with salt, so that you may know how you ought to answer everyone" (Colossians 4:5-6).

We earn the right to speak truth to power. This means, in part, that our default mode is gracious patience and gentleness.

When we speak of political engagement, we also need to think about matters of social and economic justice. When I was a seminary student, we had intense debates about the character of Christian witness that focused on whether mission was evangelism or social action. We more or less concluded that as evangelicals we believed in verbal witness and that it was the more liberal wing of the church that emphasized social action. But we must come to see that this is a false polarity, as Lesslie Newbigin put it so well: "It is clear that to set word and deed, preaching and action, against each other is absurd. . . . They mutually reinforce one another and interpret one another. Words explain the deeds, and the deeds validate the words."[2] It is a both/and. Each legitimizes the other. We witness in word *and* deed.

This means that our local churches are keenly aware of matters of justice—particularly economic justice. We cannot serve faithfully in our time without attempting to understand the economic consequences of our preaching and the ministry of the church. And this means that ministerial formation includes a basic awareness of the economics of the communities of which we are a part. Preaching that is blind to the fundamentals of the economy is naive at best. At worst, we may be actually complicit in unjust economic structures and systems. This will come to the fore most often when it comes to advocating for those who are at the margins. We must be alert to the ethnic, racial, economic, and gender issues that so easily undercut what it means to be a just society.[3]

---

[2]Lesslie Newbigin, *The Gospel in a Pluralist Society* (Grand Rapids, MI: Eerdmans, 1989), 137.
[3]For more on this, I suggest reading Tom Nelson, *The Economics of Neighborly Love: Investing in Your Community's Compassion and Capacity* (Downers Grove, IL: InterVarsity Press, 2017).

Political engagement—as presence, through principled compromise, or as we speak truth to power—is always an intentionally spiritual act. Therefore, we enter into the public square with a disposition of discernment. We are in shared or common space—the city—with an attentiveness to spiritual dimensions of the political. We go into the world with the humility that comes out of an awareness that we do not possess the truth but merely witness to the truth. We do not presume that we are the only source of wisdom for the challenges that our society might be facing.

PEACEMAKING AND CONFLICT RESOLUTION

While the church has always been called to peacemaking, this may be a particular calling of the church in a secular society. Our communities and the society at large are caught up in conflict on so many levels that it is amazing that society still functions. Our legislative assemblies are venues of conflict and discord, not collaboration and principled compromise. To help address conflict on a national or local level, whether it be political, racial, economic, or religious, it would make sense for our clergy and lay leaders to know the skills of mediation, of fostering ways for those in conflict to come to understanding and some measure of reconciliation.[4] We can be attentive to the ways in which we can be a means of fostering peace in our homes, our church communities, in our neighborhoods, and on the national and international stage.

But we need to begin at home and with our churches. Conflict at home or in the church negates our capacity to be an instrument of peace in our world. A conflicted church is in no position to foster reconciliation and harmony in the society around us. Thus, as an essential point of departure, pastors and lay leaders need to know how to respond to the presence of conflict within their own congregations. Then we can take a hopeful posture toward the presence of conflict in our communities and countries.

---

[4]Suggested reading: George J. Mitchell, *Making Peace* (Berkeley: University of California Press, 1999), on the Northern Ireland accord; Ann Garrido, *Redeeming Conflict: 12 Habits for Christian Leaders* (Notre Dame, IN: Ave Maria Press, 2016); Susan Scott, *Difficult Conversations: How to Discuss What Matters Most* (New York: Penguin Books, 2010).

We do not need to fear conflict; it is often a sign of health. It is also often generative, reflecting the potential for new learning and new growth. We do not need to assume that conflict is invariably detrimental or destructive. But there is a big difference between generative conflict and the conflict that undercuts our capacity for genuine harmony and for working together for the common good. We can come to learn, though, that conflict can be generative and not destructive. We can, to use the language of Ann Garrido, "redeem conflict." To redeem conflict means at least four things.

First, we have to name the wrong—tell the story of what has happened. Canadians, for example, can acknowledge the horror of the residential schools for indigenous children. They can recognize the profound wrong that Japanese immigrants experienced during the Second World War, when they were rounded up into internment camps and lost their property and their businesses. Citizens of the United States can name the reality of slavery and how it continues to be an achingly vivid scar in their shared psyche. Germans can own rather than deny the spectacular tragedy of the Holocaust. Israelis can recognize that it was a problem and remains a problem that so many Palestinians lost their homes and means of livelihood so that the state of Israel could be created. Serbian Christians can name the inexcusable grief that their military caused in Sarajevo and throughout present-day Bosnia during the Yugoslav Wars of the 1990s. Yes, we will move on; yes, we will make peace. But it begins with naming and not repressing the memory of what has happened.

Second, peacemaking means that we foster the capacity to move beyond being victims. Conflict almost always means there was an injustice, potentially a very significant wrong done, by one people against another. Peace is possible only if there is the capacity to leave that wrong in the past—yes, we name the wrong, but then we ask what it means to move on. It is not a matter of ignoring history, but of understanding what happened and what, if any, reparations need to be considered and implemented. It is only a cheap "peace" if we do not link peace with justice. But then, our primary identity is not that we are victims; our primary mode of engagement with the other is not through the lens of the wrong that has been done against us.

Third, we ask, "What is the way we can live *now* with justice and generosity?" Our frame of reference is the future—our children and our children's children. We ask where tensions and polarizations or deep wrongs have driven a wedge between us. We ask what it would look like and feel like if we were living at peace, with no winners and losers but only winners. We spend time thinking about what new dynamic can shape our common lives so that our children can live at peace with each other and work together for the well-being of our churches, our neighborhoods, and our countries.

Fourth, we need to remember that peace is tenuous at first; it must be tended. We need to be very intentional and present to each other; those who were in conflict need to find ways to strengthen the points of connection that would then minimize the chance of breaking the peace. We acknowledge that peace begins with small steps in the right direction while we work, slowly but surely, toward greater trust, greater mutual understanding, and a growing appreciation of the experience and journey of the other. All the while, we remain alert to the ways in which old hurts can suddenly resurface and aspects of the conflict can reemerge, perhaps inadvertently.

An exquisite example of this form of missional engagement from the position of a minority presence is that of the Arab Baptist Theological Seminary in Monsourieh, Lebanon (outside of Beirut) through its Institute for Middle Eastern Studies. Under the leadership of Dr. Martin Accad, they have used their connections to create a space for people from diverse communities with historically strained relationships to talk and eat together, to explore challenging issues and create mutual understanding. Lebanon is potentially a laboratory for Christians in other parts of the world, as within a small region that has a history of a civil war they can bring together Muslims—Sunni and Shia—and Druze community members along with Catholic, Orthodox, Presbyterian, and Baptist Christians to talk about their shared vision and aspiration for the future of Lebanon.

In Beirut, I heard Muslim, Druze, and Christian young people talk about their experience of being in a small cohort with an agenda to create understanding, to share dreams for the future of a diverse Lebanon, and, most of all, to cultivate relationships that would mitigate against any possibility of a future civil war. What was most moving to me was that these were young people whose parents had been enemies, but they were refusing to let the past determine the future. Under the leadership and mentoring of Baptist Christian leaders, they were forming a new basis for living at peace and flourishing together as friends.

It is significant to observe that the leadership for this initiative came from those at the margins, not those in positions of power or major public influence. Indeed, perhaps it was because they were a minority, because they were not the power brokers in Lebanese society, that they were positioned to be moderators of the conversation, fostering the capacity for a new generation of young people to know what it is to live at peace with their neighbor.

LEADING FROM THE MARGINS

In every aspect of our missional engagement in a secular age, we lead not from a position of power but from the margins. That is, we need to learn to lead when we may not hold the social and political levers of power. We might wish it otherwise, yet this is our social, cultural, and religious location. So why not turn from a posture of assuming that we cannot have a positive influence because we have no power, hunkering down and "making the best of it," and instead actually *leverage* the margin— precisely as the margin? Why not embrace this location in ways that are fruitful and redemptive?

Leading from the margins is something that is learned. In a fascinating essay, "Tempered Radicalism and the Politics of Ambivalence and Change," Debra E. Meyerson and Maureen A. Scully ask: What does it mean to effect change when you do not have power and influence?[5] What does it mean to have a dual identity where you are part of an organization, perhaps a country or a church, but also have an alternate affiliation or loyalty? You are at the margins in that you cannot enthusiastically share the values, the rhetoric, or the narrative of the country, church, or organization of which you are a part. What does it mean to effect

---

[5]Debra E. Meyerson and Maureen A. Scully, "Tempered Radicalism and the Politics of Ambivalence and Change," *Organizational Science* 6.5 (September–October 1995): 509-601.

positive change and make a constructive difference from the position of the minority voice or, perhaps, the position of limited influence?

Meyerson and Scully challenge the assumption that we can make a difference only if we have power to make things happen. They observe that "it is always tempting to wait until one has yet more formal power and security and can *really* effect change."[6] This might not come anytime soon, if at all. So we need to learn what it means to lead and influence from the margins. This is precisely what it means to be the church in this time and in this place. We need to learn how to do this if we want to be instruments of grace and wisdom within our social context.

From Meyerson and Scully we learn to live hopefully and generously, even at the margins. We can be a minority presence that does in the end make a difference. It will perhaps be over an extended period of time, and it may only be through seeds planted or watered that do not bear fruit right away, but if we are patient and remain hopeful and leverage the points of influence that are given to us, change will come. They urge us to think "long arc," which means that we have to cultivate the virtue of patience.

Meyerson and Scully write about organizations, with no particular attention to matters of religion, but what they say next has direct bearing on what it means to develop leaders for the church in a secular society. They insist that we must remain true to ourselves and our own values and identity, but we also should accept the *limits* of our position in the organization or, for the church, within a secular society. This means that we are not purists or idealists. We know the art of principled compromise. This does *not* mean we have lost the strength of our convictions. It is merely that we choose our battles carefully, we accept that small wins or victories do matter, and we recognize that in many respects our mere presence in the organization or country or church or society is a source of encouragement to others, including our "allies"—others who are also at the margins.

Meyerson and Scully speak of "outsiders within," who have a dual identity that is not a reflection of a lack of conviction or conscience.

---

[6]Meyerson and Scully, "Tempered Radicalism," 593.

Those in this position are not hypocrites; they are not two-faced; they are not lacking in personal integrity. They are true to themselves and their conscience—including, of course, their core values. But they are still at the margins and are resolved, as best as they can, to be generous and gracious participants in the life of the whole entity of which they are a part. They are true to themselves, but also resist thinking in terms of "us versus them"; they turn from the temptation to demonize the other. They always sustain and insist on the human connection.

Those in this position know how to use insider language to build bridges and foster understanding, doing so to assure those within the organization that they are not rebels or disaffected or unwilling to work within the system. But their language also has within it the seeds of those values and commitments, those convictions or perspectives, that need to be spoken for the well-being of the organization as a whole.

This dual identity brings a continuous tension, but we can live in the liminal space of ambiguity and tension with a spirit of generosity toward others. Those in this position know the rules and live by them; they speak when there is opportunity and choose their words carefully, not needing to or presuming to challenge the central or dominant voices each time they speak. They learn, as Emily Dickinson would say, to "tell all the truth but tell it slant." They speak in ways that plant seeds, that let understanding grow in a way that is organic and does not create undue resistance. Perhaps this means that those at the margins can learn especially from poets and other artists whose influence is always a little more subtle and, perhaps, indirect.

In all of this, we learn to appreciate the significance of "small wins." Meyerson and Scully note that it is important to choose battles well, urging their readers to tend to actions and movements that may seem to be small but are the right steps or merely one step in the right direction. The genius of a small win is that it is often not viewed as a threat to the status quo, and those who may not support it do not feel like they, in turn, have lost. Those who lead from the margins always keep the long view in mind; they are not revolutionaries but believe in gradual increments.

CONCLUSION

Missional engagement in a post-Christian secular society will be marked, at the very least, by the following: The church itself will be, in the language of Lesslie Newbigin, the hermeneutic of the gospel. It will not just speak the gospel but actually witness to the reign of Christ by living out what it means to be a people in whom the gospel is embodied.

The church will engage its social context through being present, through political engagement, and in response to opportunities to be agents of peacemaking. This does not mean that the proclamation of good news and the invitation to join the community of disciples who live under the authority of Christ will be any less present. When I was a young person, we had an evening service every Sunday that was all about evangelism. The preaching engaged those who had not made a commitment, and the service ended with an invitation to raise the hand and come forward and be prayed with to receive Christ as Lord. While that form might have had its place, evangelism will necessarily look different in a secular and pluralist society. It will be more understated and less overt. This is not because of a lack of courage or conviction on the part of the church but rather comes from a recognition that the Spirit's work in this context looks and feels different. As much as anything, it will happen alongside the life and witness of the church that is just being the church.

Sunday worship will focus on Christ, and those who are "on the way" will be welcomed to join in. They will not be the focus; Christ remains the focus. However strange the journey at first, they will come to know, over time, that Christ is present and that this presence is benevolent. Catechesis and shared learning will mark the journey to faith as much as life in the faith. Evangelism and catechesis will be fundamentally linked—so much so that they are indistinguishable.

The witness of the church to the world will be marked by an evangelism in word that only has legitimacy because Christians are salt and light in the world—we preach for Monday morning—and advocate for those at the margins, and are committed to be mediators and peacemakers. Along the way, we will be asked to give a reason for the hope that is within us. Evangelism, in other words, will always be located within a liturgical, catechetical, and missional community.

Through all of these competencies there is a constant thread: the capacity to sustain hope and to be a source of encouragement. The key is the capacity for hopeful realism. It is not about an unbounded optimism that fails to see the fragmentation around us and the innumerable setbacks and points of disappointment. It names reality but always does so with a keen awareness of the possibilities of grace. This is the genius of the exilic prophets, and it is an essential capacity for those who give leadership for the church in a secular age—whether in leading worship, or through their teaching, or in the ways that they equip the faith community for engagement with their world.

11

ECUMENISM IN A SECULAR AGE

A THEOLOGICAL CONVICTION,
A PRACTICAL NECESSITY

WHEN WE ASK WHAT IT MEANS to give leadership to the church in a secular age, it does not take long before we recognize that no one church community or denomination has all the wisdom needed for being all that we are called to be. We need one another. The imperative of church unity has always been there as a matter of theological conviction. Division has always been a major concern; it compromises the witness of the church both locally and globally. But in a post-Christian secular age, it is also a matter of *practical* necessity. Thus, leaders for the church in this context will need to learn what it means to work effectively with other Christian communities—that is, to be intentionally ecumenical.

THE EXPERIENCE AND WITNESS OF DIETRICH BONHOEFFER

When it comes to the priority and potential of ecumenism in a secular age, it is fruitful to consider the experience of Dietrich Bonhoeffer, who faced an extraordinary challenge with the rise of National Socialism in 1930s Germany.

In his biography of Bonhoeffer, Charles Marsh tells of how the young Dietrich went on a journey to Italy with his brother Klaus. Journeys to Italy were a family tradition going back to his great-grandfather, who had visited Italy upwards of twenty times in the early nineteenth century.[1] On this trip, Bonhoeffer was in Rome for Holy Week. He attended Mass

---

[1]Charles Marsh, *Strange Glory: A Life of Dietrich Bonhoeffer* (New York: Alfred A. Knopf), 20-21.

at Saint Peter's on Palm Sunday morning and then headed across the Tiber to the Church of the Gesù, which housed the crypt of Saint Ignatius Loyola. Later that day he headed up the Spanish Steps to vespers at Trinità dei Monti. The experience—in its three parts—had a lasting impression on him. As Bonhoeffer observed in his personal journal: "It was the first day on which something of the reality of Catholicism began to dawn on me."[2]

He stayed through the week, back at Saint Peter's on Holy Thursday and then Good Friday. He had come to Italy with the standard critique of the Protestant Reformation: that Catholicism has lost its way and was no longer a living expression of the ancient faith. As Marsh puts it, part of the cultural inheritance of German Protestantism was a deep suspicion if not abhorrence of all things Catholic.[3] But clearly Bonhoeffer emerged from this trip to Italy with a more open heart and mind. He was humbled as he entered into a vibrant and living exemplar of the ancient faith. It touched him to the core.[4] The most enduring impression from this trip to Italy was "the universality of the church."[5]

One of the most significant consequences was that going forward Bonhoeffer's theology and spirituality did not fall into the usual Protestant-Catholic divide. Marsh calls him a "natural ecumenist."[6] What emerged for him was a capacity to draw on wisdom from wherever he could find it and a resistance to framing his own theology in light of the sixteenth-century disputes. This capacity is simply crucial to the ability of the church to engage a secular context. We need the perspectives of the other; none of us have all the wisdom we need, and the sixteenth-century debates often blind us to these potentially new and essential sources of insight.

Leaning into and learning from Catholic sources was not the only way in which Bonhoeffer stepped out of his traditional German Lutheran world. While in the New York City a few years later, he entered into the world of African American Baptist theology and worship, dropping into

---

[2]Marsh, *Strange Glory*, 30.
[3]Marsh, *Strange Glory*, 406.
[4]Marsh, *Strange Glory*, 30-31.
[5]Marsh, *Strange Glory*, 30.
[6]Marsh, *Strange Glory*, 44.

opportunities for worship in Baptist churches in Harlem. This was a very different world from that of his youth and was, again, marked by a vibrant faith and spirituality.[7] He was not merely captivated by Catholic worship or sensibilities per se; he was willing to see authentic faith and learn from it wherever it was found. He did not convert to Italian Catholicism or join an African American Baptist church, but he knew that both were authentic expressions of what it means to be the church.

It is his Catholic engagement that is of particular note in that, years later, his most enduring and well-known publication, *Life Together*, could only have emerged from someone who recognized the enduring wisdom and significance of the Rule of Saint Benedict. Notably, he was accused—by Karl Barth and others—of being a little too "Catholic" in this publication on account of his attempts to bring a rule of life and a quasi-monastic rhythm to life in community at Finkenwalde, the seminary he established in what was then northeast Germany.

Toward the end of his life, in danger of being arrested, he found a home—both a spiritual home and a place of physical rest and distance for prayer and writing—in the Benedictine monastery in the village of Ettal, south of Munich. There he finished the manuscript for *Ethics*, which would be published posthumously. It is an exquisite testimony that the most important theological contribution of this extraordinary Lutheran theologian was written in the safety of a Catholic monastery where he took his meals, attended Mass even though he could not take communion, and came, as he put it in his journal, to pray for all churches, Roman and Protestant.[8] Then, in an amazing full circle, Bonhoeffer gave back. While a prisoner, immediately prior to being transported to Flossenburg where he would be executed, he led morning worship for a group of fellow prisoners, most of whom were Catholic.[9]

Along the way, Bonhoeffer was active within the burgeoning ecumenical movement of the 1920s and '30s. In 1933 he was in England and met George Bell, the Anglo-Catholic bishop of Chichester whom Bonhoeffer had first heard speak at an ecumenical conference the year before.

---

[7] Marsh, *Strange Glory*, 116.
[8] Marsh, *Strange Glory*, 298-99.
[9] Marsh, *Strange Glory*, 389.

They eventually formed a friendship that was vital to Bonhoeffer when he became increasingly disillusioned with the German Protestant churches. Thus when Bonhoeffer was not getting the support and encouragement he needed from his own church, he looked elsewhere, whether to German Catholicism or to English Anglican connections. He felt and knew that he could not face on his own the challenges he was encountering, and spoke in an essay of his appreciation for this external support and prayer.[10] In thinking theologically about the meaning of ecumenism he realized that the Confessing Church in Germany had a certain accountability to the larger Christian community and reflected on what authority, if any, was housed within the ecumenical movement.[11] He insisted on the universality of the church with diverse expressions of the "riches and harmony of Christendom," as he put it, and concluded: "None has a claim to sole validity, each brings its own special gift and does its own special service for the whole; truth lies only in unity."[12]

He was a beneficiary of the ecumenical movement and also invested back, asking difficult theological questions about the ecclesial significance of ecumenism and wondering about the challenge that churches outside of Germany had as they sought to relate to two different (and, in some degrees, opposing) German Lutheran churches. He did not sentimentalize what it meant to believe in the church, and he certainly recognized that it was a challenge to foster ecumenical relations. But it was worth the time and effort, because ecumenism was for him not only a matter of theological conviction but also a practical necessity. He demonstrates that we need to speak to both the theological conviction and the practical necessity of ecumenism in a secular age.

ECUMENISM: THE THEOLOGICAL CONVICTION

First, and most fundamentally, we need to affirm the universality of the church. This is a matter of creedal conviction: we believe in one, holy, catholic, and apostolic church.

---

[10]Dietrich Bonhoeffer, *No Rusty Swords: Letters, Lectures and Notes 1928–1936*, trans. John Bowden, ed. Edwin H. Robertson, Collected Works 1 (London: Collins, 1958), 323.

[11]Bonhoeffer, *No Rusty Swords*, 324-25.

[12]Bonhoeffer, *No Rusty Swords*, 330.

Growing up in Latin America I was part of a Christian community that was firmly "evangelical," which meant: not Catholic; not pentecostal. Our pastor was not ambivalent on this score. On any given Sunday we could count on him to point one direction to the Catholic cathedral or the other to the "Templo Pentecostal" (the Pentecostal Temple) and remind us of the error of *their* ways. As young people, we would be curious who it would be this Sunday; would he point to his right and condemn the Catholics or would he point to his left and speak to the dangers of the charismatics? We would joke that on special Sundays he would denounce both; this was our idea of a high feast!

What emerged from this way of thinking when it came to other church groups is that we defined ourselves as over against the presumed errors of the other. Thus anything that even seemly remotely Catholic was to be avoided: no candles, nothing that seemed to indicate any possibility that the sacraments might be a means of grace, nothing by way of visuals or paintings on the walls. I could go on; we had quite the list. And it was not just the Catholics; my father was at one point censured for attending a wedding at a Lutheran church because the Lutherans had not sufficiently rejected the "superstitious sacramentality" of Rome. As for the pentecostals, we assiduously avoided anything that might indicate that the Holy Spirit was active and present in any kind of immediate way. The Holy Spirit had inspired the Bible, centuries ago, and now the Spirit was at most present to help us understand the Bible.

This might all seem rather quaint now, but recently I heard of an evangelical church where some members were saying that their church was becoming "too Catholic" because they were exploring the possibility of celebrating the Lord's Table more frequently. When I heard this, I was stunned by what seemed the continued proclivity to assume that the way we are and have always been is all we need. Are we still defining ourselves over against the other?

Few things are more crucial to the church in our day as that we find a way, with the help of the Holy Spirit, to live in unity. Both locally and globally, we need to know the grace of genuine Christian fellowship across the divide of diverse Christian traditions. Our capacity, as Christian communities, to witness in word and deed to the reign of

Christ requires that we live in unity that is evident to the communities and cities in which we live. In other words, ecumenicity has always been basic to what it means to be the church. This is particularly so in a post-Christian world. The church in the West will only have credibility if it learns what it means to live in unity. But more, it will only have the capacity to do this as we learn and work with those of other Christian traditions.

This will require a theological formulation of what it means to affirm unity and diversity around a common confession. We are past longing for or actively seeking an organizational unity. Rather, we seek a unity that transcends anything institutional; we are not after an administrative structure that will somehow hold us together. Rather, the unity to which we are called in our generation is one that values diversity and difference, and yet, through all that diversity, finds an uncanny unity that is a source of strength and vibrant missional witness. Indeed, as Father Thomas Ryan would observe, our diversity is not a problem but something in which we should actually rejoice.[13]

This affirmation of diversity will lead us to recognize where there might be wisdom housed within another church tradition or spiritual heritage that might be invaluable for us. Rather than defining ourselves as over against the other, we learn from and lean into the wisdom that the other brings to the table.

ECUMENISM: A PRACTICAL NECESSITY

All of this is part of the essential theological work of reflecting on what it means to be the church and how unity with diversity is a mark of strength. But we need to go further and recognize that in a secular age, ecumenism is not merely a matter of theological conviction but also a *practical* necessity. We have come a long way in the ecumenical movement in an appreciation of what for Bonhoeffer spoke of as "the universality of the church." We know that we cannot define what it means to be the church solely by the criteria of our own theological and spiritual

---

[13]Thomas Ryan, *Christian Unity: How You Can Make a Difference* (New York: Paulist Press, 2015). See also Luder G. Whitlock Jr., *Divided We Fall: Overcoming a History of Christian Disunity* (Phillipsburg, NJ: P&R, 2017).

communities of faith. We know that there is genuine faith in the hearts of those within other communions. We have known these things, but now we need to tend and care for what is given to us.

Stefan Paas, writing from the perspective of the Dutch Reformed church, observes: "In a highly secularized context, it is extremely damaging for the mission of the church if Christian leaders fight each other in public over issues that no non-Christian understands."[14] In other words, the lack of unity discredits the gospel and the witness of the Spirit to that gospel. But then he goes further and stresses that we need to establish what he calls "practices of ecclesial unity."[15] Making a difference *ecumenically* is an essential capacity for leadership in the church in a secular age. This is learned; it requires resolve and intentional investment of time and energy to cultivate the capacities to do it well. As Thomas Ryan has stated it:

> The training and preparation of leaders in the ecumenical movement cannot be left to chance. The movement needs a new generation of ecumenical practitioners who are aware of the break-throughs of the past and who have a fire in their hearts to carry those advances forward into the future and build upon them.[16]

Ryan further references the great line in "Ways to Community" (1980), from the Lutheran-Roman Catholic Dialogue: "Ecumenical awareness needs to be developed by permeating *theological education* with ecumenism."[17]

Seminaries need to ask: Does our program of theological formation anticipate challenges and opportunities for ecumenical connections? Do our graduating students have the requisite vision for ecumenism and the capacity for fostering Christian unity? When they accept a new pastoral or ministerial appointment, will they early on consider the ways in which they could be a positive agent for fellowship and learning across denominational lines? Individual or local faith communities will not likely

---

[14]Stefan Paas, *Church Planting in the Secular West: Learning from the European Experience* (Grand Rapids, MI: Eerdmans, 2016), 109.

[15]Paas, *Church Planting*, 109.

[16]Ryan, *Christian Unity*, 130.

[17]Ryan, *Christian Unity*, 130 (emphasis Ryan's).

actively pursue Christian unity if their clergy are not on board, embracing this vision.

Encouraged by the example of Dietrich Bonhoeffer, I would note three essential competencies—what Stefan Paas calls "practices of ecclesial unity." Each of these is surely essential to the theological formation of leaders for the church in our time.

Learning with and from one another. We are not going to navigate this complicated world without realizing that the wisdom for our time comes as we attend to each other, learning from each other and with each other—what has aptly been called "receptive ecumenism." We need to be in conversation with those of other theological traditions. Theological education and the formation of leadership for Christian communities should, of course, be located within a particular theological and spiritual heritage. Yet we can do this in a way that is not framed over against those with whom our forefathers and foremothers differed, but as a way to appreciate the particulars of our own heritage. We locate, humbly, our own heritage, but do not assume that it is the gold standard or define our own theological vision through the lens of schisms and debates.

This also means that we will be reading other sources and learning from other traditions. As a seminary student in the 1970s, I did not read a single Catholic. While we did read Lesslie Newbigin, we did not read mainline theologians until my last semester, when we read a little Karl Barth and a smattering of liberation theologians as a modest attempt to alert us to other perspectives.

That is simply not an option in the current context. The spiritual resources on which we will draw will certainly include the insights and admonitions from our respective theological and spiritual traditions: Wesleyans will read Wesley; Mennonites will read Anabaptist sources; Reformed church leaders will be reading spiritual guides in that tradition. But we will also learn to draw on wisdom from each other's wells—with Catholic Christians reading Luther and Calvin, evangelicals reading John of the Cross and Teresa of Ávila, and Christians who are heirs of the Western church—Catholic and Protestant—reading Orthodox writers. If we are studying the meaning of the sacraments, for example, we need to be reading "Baptism, Eucharist and Ministry" (1982), one of the great ecumenical documents. Catholics might find value in reading Calvin on the meaning of the Eucharist. Catholics and evangelical Protestants have much to gain by reading the Orthodox perspective that emerges in Alexander Schmemann's *For the Life of the World*. We all might come to appreciate our own traditions in light of this broader conversation.

Our various tribes and ecclesial communities also need to read the church fathers and mothers to gain wisdom from the pre-Christendom church. Rather than define our theological education in terms of schisms—between East and West, between the Protestant and Catholic Reformations, between the magisterial and radical Reformation, between Anabaptists and others of the northern Reformation, or between mainline and evangelical—we lean more intentionally into the wisdom of the early church.

In our programs of theological formation, we should learn side by side with people from other traditions. We will take courses together and our professors will come from diverse traditions. Where this is not possible, we will have guest lecturers and chapel speakers that bring us into a learning mode with those from other theological and spiritual traditions. In the process, we will likely disagree on significant matters, and we will not apologize for where we differ and for the diverse theological convictions and perspectives that we bring to the table. But we will do so with humility, recognizing that sincere and smart women and men in other churches and denominations see things differently.

The invitation to joint witness. In addition to shared learning, we also have to learn what it means to cultivate the capacity for shared *witness*. That is, we learn how to work and serve collaboratively—with the give and take of carrying the load together, of serving together, while all along refusing to presume that anyone should take credit from our joint efforts.

This means that together, in our cities and social locations, we consciously identify those opportunities for missional engagement where we need one another to help us carry the load and accomplish something worthwhile. That is, we look for challenges that we know are simply too big for any one of us and come together, arm in arm, to see in what ways we can make a difference—whether it is homelessness within our cities, the opioid crisis that is tearing families apart, or the challenge of welcoming immigrants and refugees into our communities.

I think, for example, of the series of European ecumenical assemblies that considered how the ecumenical movement could leverage its connections toward shared, visible, and concrete work in creation care—fostering, together, greater environmental stewardship. Or, on a more local level, one cannot help but be impressed with the coordinated effort to confront the payday loan industry in Texas. Catholics, Southern Baptists, and Cooperative Baptists came together and leveraged the weight of their joint influence to make a substantive difference in the lives of the poor within their communities.[18]

Praying for one another. Third, surely the formation of leadership for the church in our day will necessarily include cultivating, by example and by commendation, prayer for the unity of the church. A few years ago I was asked to bring the Sunday morning sermon at Southview Alliance Church in Calgary, Alberta. What a delight it was when we came in the liturgy to the prayers of the people and offered prayers for all the other congregations in that part of the city—Catholic, Baptist, Mennonite, and pentecostal. This was deeply encouraging, but it was also formative. It is a crucial form of leadership that cultivates a more ecumenical and generous disposition within our faith communities.

CONCLUSION

This is not easy work. We may have theological convictions about unity and diversity and the importance of ecumenism, but there is so much that is challenging and discouraging. Each of us will experience different forms of resistance. Thus we always need to find ways and means to encourage one another, such that, in the words of the apostle Paul from the letter to the Galatians: "Let us not grow weary in doing what is right, for we will reap at harvest time, if we do not give up. So then, whenever we have an opportunity, let us work for the good of all, and especially for those of the family of faith" (Galatians 6:9-10).

---

[18]A documentary film that tells this story is *The Ordinance: Texas Churches vs. the Payday Loan Industry*, Deidox Films (2016), https://deidox.org/theordinance.

12

CULTIVATING INTERIORITY

SPIRITUAL PRACTICE IN A SECULAR AGE

WHEN WE CONSIDER WHAT IT MEANS to give leadership for the church in a secular age, we need to cultivate certain capacities, competencies, and commitments. But all of this will be for naught if we do not foster the *internal* dispositions—ways of seeing, thinking, and feeling—that support and sustain the ways in which we function as leaders. This matter of our interior life must be addressed against the backdrop of certain assumptions. First, we are going to live and lead the church with grace and courage in this time and in this place; we are going to be very *present* to our circumstances. It may not be the world as we wish it to be, but that is not the point. This is the world that is before us.

Then also, we recognize that we live and work and serve Christ in a context that is in a constant state of flux. In this highly fluid context, we must have a fixed point that gives clarity and orientation to our lives and thus to our work and the leadership we are called on to provide. My observation is that this cannot merely be a conviction about truth, however vital and important that may be. Rather, it needs to be a person—the risen and ascended Christ. Our reference point is not so much theology as an existential and dynamic connection, in real time, with the One who sits on the throne of the universe. I'll get to this later in the chapter, but first I need to set the stage.

THE FEAR FACTOR

It has become apparent to almost every spiritual writer of our generation that the greatest threat that the church faces in a secular age is not something external to it—not secularism, Islam, or any other "ism" or external agent—but something internal, namely, fear. W. H. Auden was prescient when in 1947 he published his magisterial poem *The Age of Anxiety*, seemingly picking up on the central theme of Søren Kierkegaard's prophetic word a century earlier in *The Concept of Anxiety*. Kierkegaard distinguished between fear and anxiety by suggesting that fear is linked to something—a definite threat—whereas anxiety is a state of simply being fearful without reference to any one thing in particular. In the time since Auden, Henri Nouwen has spoken of a "culture of fear" and suggested that fear has now become so pathologically present that it is no longer even recognized; it has come to be so part of the air we breathe that we do not even know it is there. It is a taken-for-granted part of the emotional landscape in which we live and work. Parker Palmer has added to this the challenge of our teaching and learning in that our schools and our universities are hotbeds of fear and anxiety, so much so that learning is virtually impossible.[1]

Rowan Williams concludes that we need to address the reality of fear head on. He notes that when there is a threat, a secular society has no skills for managing this threat and thus "neurotic fear has free play."[2] He notes that the European and North Atlantic world lives in a state of pervasive fear, and he lists those fears—the loss of social identity, interference from the government, massive immigration, terrorism, the influence of those who would corrupt our youth. His point is not so much whether these fears are justified; it is that they are pervasive. They are constant in our public speech; the fear is obsessive. Secular society has no capacity to look truthfully and critically at the source of this paralyzing fear.[3]

In response, Williams notes, we resort to violence and blaming others rather than taking responsibility for our own behavior. We think that military strength might ease our fears, but such a perspective only superficially alleviates the anxiety as we overestimate our capacity to change

---

[1] W. H. Auden, *The Age of Anxiety: A Baroque Eclogue* (1947); Søren Kierkegaard, *The Concept of Anxiety* (1844); Henri J. M. Nouwen, *Lifesigns: Intimacy, Fecundity, and Ecstasy in Christian Perspective* (New York: Doubleday, 1986); Parker Palmer, *The Courage to Teach* (San Francisco: Jossey-Bass, 1998).

[2] Rowan Williams, *The Truce of God* (Grand Rapids, MI: Eerdmans, 1983), 5.

[3] Williams, *Truce of God*, 10-11.

things.[4] It is not that the threats are not real; it is rather that we are not responding appropriately. The response needs to be that we take responsibility for our own lives and learn to live in radical dependence on God. For Williams, we need to ask what it means "to live and pray Christianly by way of looking at our fears and their slow corruption of our imagination."[5] Only as we address our fears can we begin to see in truth. Walter Brueggemann makes a similar observation, quoting a sermon that Karl Barth gave in 1914 prior to World War I: "Excessive preoccupation with worry and comfort is to be resisted: 'Stand back from these kinds of questions and answers. Away with them! . . . For our praying then is not real praying, no matter how eagerly we besiege God with our anxious requests.'"[6]

It is fruitful here to reference Edwin H. Friedman's 1995 publication *The Failure of Nerve: Leadership in the Age of the Quick Fix.*[7] He speaks of an imperative to be a well-differentiated leader, by which he means someone who has clarity about his or her own life goals and is "less likely to become lost in the anxious emotional processes" that are inevitable in any organization.[8] Well-differentiated leaders are connected but separate. It is not that they are emotionally disconnected or autocratic. It is, rather, that they are able to manage their own personal reactions in the midst of the anxiety that is all around them. No one does this easily, but his key point remains that effective leaders improve on their capacity to do this.

Then also, Friedman points out the danger of "sabotage" to the well-differentiated leader. He writes, "The climate of contemporary America has become so chronically anxious that our society has gone into an emotional regression that is toxic to well-defined leadership."[9] Since people want comfort rather than true leadership that challenges them, the well-differentiated leader will trigger a reaction: "It is simply not

---

[4]Williams, *Truce of God*, 17-19.

[5]Williams, *Truce of God*, ix.

[6]Walter Brueggemann, "How Karl Barth Preached the Gospel in a Time of Crisis," *Christian Century*, June 21, 2017, 37.

[7]Edwin H. Friedman, *A Failure of Nerve: Leadership in the Age of the Quick Fix* (New York: Seabury Books, 2007).

[8]Friedman, *Failure of Nerve*, 14.

[9]Friedman, *Failure of Nerve*, 53.

possible to succeed at an effort of leadership through self-differentiation without triggering reactivity."[10] The reason, of course is that good leaders do not bring false comfort; they are doing what needs to be done, and this will stir up anxiety. But we must lead in a way that helps our organizations and communities grow, mature, and be effective. This means we will be agents of change, which always stirs up anxiety. Thus Friedman writes: "The capacity of a leader to be prepared for, to be aware of, and to learn how to skillfully deal with this type of crisis [sabotage] may be the most important aspect of leadership. It is literally the key to the kingdom."[11]

It only follows, then, that we can only deal with sabotage if we are a non-anxious presence. Yes, we must be emotionally connected, but we are not caught up in the swirl of anxiety that may actually be caused by our leadership. We lead in this way not because we are trying to make people anxious but because we are initiating the changes that are needed; we choose not to let our fear or the fears of others keep us from doing what needs to be done. Thus Leo Tolstoy, in *War and Peace*, at a crucial point in the battle, slips in the line that captures it all: "The moral hesitation that decides the fate of battles . . . [is] fear."[12] Or, as Hans Urs von Balthasar has put it:

> Only a Christian who does not allow himself to be infected by modern humanity's neurotic anxiety . . . has any hope of exercising a Christian influence on this age. He will not hastily turn away from the anxiety of his fellow men and fellow Christians but will show them how to extricate themselves from their fruitless withdrawal into themselves and will point out the paths by which they can step out into the open, into faith's daring.[13]

All this is to stress that we cannot be naive about the power of fear around us. It has the potential to infiltrate our own hearts and compromise our capacity to lead.

---

[10]Friedman, *Failure of Nerve*, 246.

[11]Friedman, *Failure of Nerve*, 246-47.

[12]Leo Tolstoy, *War and Peace*, trans. Richard Pevear and Larissa Volokhonsky (New York: Alfred A. Knopf, 2007), 191.

[13]Quoted by Michael Kinnamon, *The Witness of Religion in an Age of Fear* (Louisville, KY: Westminster John Knox Press, 2017), 37-38.

THE PREREQUISITE: AN *INTENTIONAL* INTERIORITY

We will only be able to address fear in our churches or organizations—or in our society—if we come to terms with our own fears. For this, we must cultivate an interiority that is focused on the ascended Christ and that is housed in particular spiritual practices.

Consider the insight of Louis Dupré, former professor of the philosophy of religion at Yale University.[14] Dupré speaks to the secularity of our time, referencing the remark of Karl Rahner that "Christianity in the future will be mystical or it will be not at all." He then stresses that "to survive as a genuine believer, the Christian must now personally integrate what tradition did in the past."[15] I would add that the individual and the church will need to cultivate the capacity to be deeply Christian when it is not reinforced by the social context and cultural sensibilities in which they are living. We will need to develop the deeply religious sensibilities of those who know intimately what it means to abide in Christ (John 15:4) and to walk in the Spirit.

Dupré observes that this will involve developing an *interiority*—not as a way of being disengaged from our society, but as a means of gaining the spiritual resources that will equip us and empower us to actually engage in our culture. As he puts it,

> Even the contemplative is responsible for the civilization in which he or she lives. . . . A genuine Christian interiority must provide the inspiration for a humanism capable of living a vigorous, free and open life within one's culture, whatever its condition may be. . . . The spiritual Christian is not involved in constant polemics with the surrounding secular world. Since that person's force and strength comes from within, he or she can grant society and culture their full autonomy.[16]

This is a liberating observation. We are not wringing our hands or bemoaning our state, but rather—at peace with God's purposes, our world, and ourselves—we cultivate the capacity to live at peace with our world and with ourselves.

---

[14]"Seeking Christian Interiority: An Interview with Louis Dupré," *Christian Century*, July 16-23, 1997, 654-60.
[15]Dupré, "Seeking Christian Interiority," 655.
[16]Dupré, "Seeking Christian Interiority," 657.

THE ASCENSION AND CHRISTIAN INTERIORITY

In speaking about interiority, we need to be very particular regarding the *focus*. It is not merely a matter of being spiritual. Ultimately and most critically, it has as its focus the risen and ascended Christ Jesus. It is, in the language of John 15:4, about abiding in Christ as Christ abides in us—that is, that one finds one's true spiritual home not in oneself but in another, the risen Christ. Here is where we might lean into the language of the apostle when he writes: "So if you have been raised with Christ, seek the things that are above, where Christ is, seated at the right hand of God. Set your minds on things that are above, not on things that are on earth, for you have died, and your life is hidden with Christ in God" (Colossians 3:1-3).

Yes, of course, Christian spirituality at its best nurtures a strong personal identity. It fosters self-knowledge and the kind of centeredness that in some respects might seem comparable to the Buddhist notion of mindfulness, where one is at peace with oneself and one's world, content and able to engage the world without fretfulness. Without doubt, Christian spirituality at its best also cultivates a distinctive community identity so that the Christian is very much a person in community, comparable to a society or club that is marked by mutual interdependence and hospitality toward one another. But what sets apart a Christian spirituality, what makes it radically different, is the focus on Christ, who in real time is seated on the throne of the universe and who in real time is in dynamic fellowship with the church and, as I wish to make the focus here, with the individual Christian.

If we are going to provide non-anxious leadership for the church in a secular age, it is this orientation—"set your minds on things above"—that needs to become the most fundamental thing about us. Our interiority is all for naught if it only means that we are at peace with ourselves; this is not sustainable and not, ultimately, transformative. And however linked and associated we are with others, if we are not deeply and intentionally finding our true spiritual home in Christ we will easily get caught up in the fear and anxiety and even the dysfunction of the church communities of which we are a part. Community will be mere clubbiness; the fears and anxieties of the church community will invade our own hearts.

Living and leading without anxiety is not about a psychological ploy or technique. It is about meeting Christ in real time—having a personal encounter in one's prayers—where we in the inner recesses of our hearts and minds hear the words that Christ originally spoke to his disciples and now says to us: "Do not be afraid. . . . I am with you always" (Matthew 28:10, 20). If the original disciples were not afraid, it was because they lived with an existential awareness of the presence of the ascended Christ.

CHRISTIAN INTERIORITY IS "HOUSED"

This focus on Christ is nurtured by some very specific spiritual practices. These are the wineskins for the life-giving wine. They are the means to the end—the interior life—but they are an *essential* means. They are the means of grace, the practices by which we nurture and cultivate an interior life that has as its focus and goal "Christ in you the hope of glory" (Colossians 1:27).

Here is where we see the relevance of the ancient Rule of Saint Benedict or, more recently, Kierkegaard's *Training in Christianity* or Dietrich Bonhoeffer's *Life Together* or David Ford's *The Shape of Living*.[17] These contributions to the practice of the Christian life essentially appropriate ancient monastic wisdom about the forms or rhythms of the spiritual life. The wisdom of the monastic spiritual tradition has continuing relevance to the church in a secular age not because it might be duplicated—the answer to the rise of secularity is not for the church to *retreat* into monastic communities. Rather, we look to wisdom from the monastic experience so that it might be incorporated into the rhythms of life in the secular city. From it we learn habituated practices that can become part of the routines of our lives. Their fruitfulness is found not in a solitary or one-off practice but from our doing them again and again and again.

Without in any way seeking to be exhaustive, here is what might mark the patterns of life of those who would seek to live in dynamic and intentional communion with Christ in a manner that draws on this ancient wisdom: morning and evening prayer, spiritual friendship and spiritual direction, sabbath observance, and practices of embodiment. These are

---

[17]David Ford, *The Shape of Living: Spiritual Directions for Everyday Life* (Grand Rapids, MI: Baker, 1998).

merely suggestive, yet it would be difficult to commend a person for leadership for the church in this social and cultural context if they had not incorporated, in some respect, each into their daily experience.

As I review these practices, some may wonder if these are not essential for all Christians who seek to live faithfully in a pluralist and secular context. And, of course, they are for one and all. But I might stress two things: first, these are nonnegotiable for the leader; and second, leaders model these practices for those whom they serve.

Morning and evening prayers. Following Bonhoeffer's *Life Together*, I would suggest that the genius of our daily prayers is the counterpoint between our personal, solitary prayers—the daily experience of solitude with the Scriptures and the personal morning liturgies by which we begin the day with the Lord (following the brewing of the appropriate morning beverage, of course!)—and our practice of prayer in community. If and as we are able, we should commit to be part of morning prayers and compline or perhaps vespers. If and as we are able, we should be part of a community that recognizes the significance of a shared experience of ending the day together in silence and with the prayers that commend our souls to God as we move into the darkness and the sleep that marks the night.

Our personal prayers will be marked by contemplation; in our praying we dwell in the presence of Christ. The contemplative life is nonnegotiable. It is truly the only way that we can navigate an age of anxiety such that, as noted already, we personally behold Christ with the eyes of our hearts and hear Christ assure us that we are loved and that we do not need to be afraid. As Rowan Williams puts it bluntly: "Contemplation is . . . an ontological necessity."[18]

Both our personal prayers and our prayers in community will be marked by the Psalms—prayed as our prayers, the prayers of God's people praying with Christ. We will pray through the Psalms systematically, from lament to comfort, from anger to courage, from fear to faith.

---

[18]Rowan Williams, *A Silent Action: Engagements with Thomas Merton*, (Louisville, KY: Fons Vitae, 2011), 30. That statement is part of the fuller articulation, "Contemplation is not a religious exercise but an ontological necessity in the intense *personalism* of Christian faith" (Williams's emphasis).

We will be women and men whose interior life is deeply shaped by the psalter.

And then also, our personal and daily prayers should necessarily include the simple practice of "care casting"—where, in the language of Philippians 4, we are anxious for nothing but, leaning also into the call of 1 Peter 5, we cast our cares on him who cares for us. This then leaves us with the peace that transcends all understanding (Philippians 4:8).

Spiritual direction and spiritual friendship. Even though the Christian interior life is ultimately our own journey and is, in many respects, a solitary journey, it is not one that we can presume to undertake alone. One of the great threats to the spiritual life is that it can become so solitary that we do not even know what is happening in our own souls. The genius of being in community, in part, is that we avoid the potential for narcissism: other significant players in our lives provide both accountability and encouragement.

Yes, our deep orientation is toward Christ, the ascended Lord. But we cannot be in fellowship with Christ if we are not living *accountable* to others for our interior life and if we are not on the journey in the company of others who are a source of encouragement in the face of difficulty and challenge. By "others," I mean those in our lives—and they do not need to be many—with whom there is no pretense, no posturing, no need to impress. Our conversations, whether formal or "along the way," are marked by an attentiveness to the emotional contours of our lives in that we speak about our joys and sorrows with a liberating honesty.

The friend or director or pastor is the other in our lives who has the capacity and courage to speak with love, generosity, and courage and thus help us tend to the interior witness of the Spirit in times of stress, discouragement, and decision-making. They do not presume to speak for God, but they keep us attentive to the Spirit, and they keep us faithful to our own commitments and confession.

By "spiritual friendship" I am suggesting that we should have a peer who is on the journey with you, walking together in mutual conversation. Shared meals and walks become opportunities for reflecting together on the journey of faith. By "spiritual direction" I refer to someone who has formal training as a pastor or director—potentially but not necessarily a generation older—with whom the primary character of the relationship is to reflect in a focused and intentional manner on your spiritual journey and how the Spirit is present to that journey.[19]

Sabbath observance. Could it be that sabbath observance might be one of the key markers of the church and of the Christian community in a secular age? Sabbath observance is an essential point of demarcation wherein the Christian community signals an orientation to Christ as Creator and Redeemer rather than to the gods of the age, the gods of the mall and consumerism and frenetic business. Perhaps you observe it with flexibility because of your work situation, so that one week the Sabbath for you might be on Saturday and another week it might have to shift because of a Saturday obligation.

It might also be the case that in a culture of fear one of the most powerful antidotes is the regular but simple (if only it were so simple!) practice of Sabbath disengagement. Sabbath is fundamentally a day in which we refuse to worry. We rest from our work; we set aside the cares of work, of family, of the nation-states of which we are a part, and we rest in the confidence that all is well and will be well. Sabbath is, in many respects, the ultimate declaration that Christ is the ascended Lord who sits on the throne of the universe. It is an act of faith in that there is so much that is wrong in the world, so much that *needs* to be done, and so much that *could* be done. But we rest in the grace and power of God and refuse, at least for this day, to carry the cares of this world. One day in seven, we set them aside.

Practices of embodiment. Finally, we need to speak more broadly about spiritual practices that involve the body. Living in fellowship with the ascended Christ is not merely an interior matter; it is interior, but it is an interiority that is deeply and intentionally *embodied*.

Consider, for example, the physical routines or practices that draw us into the rhythms of the created order. Perhaps it is gardening, or the work of the amateur carpenter or woodworker, or the craft of making quilts or

---

[19]There are many resources on the ministry of spiritual direction, including my own publication that seeks to collate the wisdom that has emerged about this ancient and contemporary form of pastoral presence in the life of another. See Gordon T. Smith, *Spiritual Direction: A Guide for Giving and Receiving Direction* (Downers Grove, IL: InterVarsity Press, 2014).

embroidery. Or it might be bricklaying or building stone walls and terraces, or weaving—resting in the rhythmic sound of the loom as an exquisite piece of fabric emerges. All these are simple but regular practices of working with our hands, tending to beauty and the order of creation.

We also might come to learn the power and grace of walking. Of course, we could draw on the ancient practice of pilgrimage and procession, but here I am thinking in particular of walking and hiking our neighborhoods, our cities, and the wilderness areas on the periphery of our cities.[20] We do not need to add to our carbon footprint by heading to some exotic location to do a spiritual pilgrimage; we can walk our own towns and cities and the areas nearby. In walking we can feel the ground, and in moving at this pace—as opposed to that of a car or train, and especially that of an airplane—we are free to attend to the sounds of children in a school playground, the birds in their morning and evening song, or two neighbors chatting about life and work and the grandkids. Walking anchors us, locates us, grounds us, and thus embodies us. It slows us down and moderates the heart, which so easily descends into anxiety.

However, when it comes to practices of embodiment, nothing is more crucial and nothing more fundamental than regular—meaning frequent *and* regular—participation in the Lord's Supper. The ancient wisdom on this score is straightforward: the Eucharist is bread for the road; the Eucharist is a real-time encounter with the risen Lord; the Eucharist is the renewal of hope. If other practices are optional, this practice is mandated. As with contemplation (as noted in the line from Rowan Williams above), the Lord's Table is an *ontological* necessity.

---

[20]See Belden C. Lane, *The Solace of Fierce Landscapes: Exploring Desert and Mountain Spirituality* (New York: Oxford University Press, 1998), especially chapter 1, page 11. See also the fine memoir and reflection on walking, *The Road Is How: A Prairie Pilgrimage Through Nature, Desire and Soul* (New York: Harper Perennial, 2014) by Trevor Herriot, who makes a persuasive argument that we should learn to walk our own neighborhoods and surrounding landscapes rather than heading off on "exotic" pilgrimages. My wife and I have delighted in a book that was gifted us when we moved to Calgary titled *Calgary's Best Hikes and Walks*. It has been a joy to walk the back streets, parks, ravines, and major avenues with this little book as our guide, with suggested routes brilliantly planned in such a way that we consistently end up near one of Calgary's superb coffee shops. See also the delightful call to walking by Mark Buchanan, *God Walk: Moving at the Speed of Your Soul* (Grand Rapids, MI: Zondervan, 2020).

To my more evangelical and nonliturgical sisters and brothers I say that, in a post-Christian secular society, once a month may not be enough. It will not cut through the deep anxiety that so frequently invades our hearts. It will not be frequent enough to actually be the means by which we live, as the basic orientation of our lives, toward Christ ascended. We need to be at the Table often so that, through regular practice, we are present again and again to the ascended Christ so that this posture and disposition becomes truly a habit of the heart. There is simply no justification whatsoever for a church or denomination to claim, out of some perverse fear that this will seem Catholic, that their tradition does not believe in more frequent celebration of the Lord's Supper.

Perhaps we need to get over our denominational assumptions and start over. The book of Acts indicates that the early church celebrated the Table each time they gathered (Acts 20:7). The patristic voices likewise all assume weekly practice of the Lord's Table. For non-Catholics, non-Orthodox, or non-Anglicans, we can go to Calvin or Wesley and note their presumption that more frequent observance makes deep sense, and in the process consider afresh why this meal matters so much. In his exquisite sermon "The Duty of Constant Communion," John Wesley calls for being at the Lord's Table as often as possible.[21] It was his personal practice to be at the Table twice a week—on Sundays, of course, but also on Thursdays. It was the practice of his time that Anglican churches typically held a noon hour celebration of the Lord's Supper on Thursdays.

Congregations that take seriously the call to the church to be a nonanxious presence in a secular age and in a culture of fear will celebrate the Lord's Table weekly. And leaders who long to dwell in and with Christ, as the mark and pattern of their lives, will find ways by which they can take communion even more frequently. During Lent, for example, they could drop in at the local Anglican church that perhaps has daily communion in this season of the year. They could scan the neighborhood and see who has midweek celebrations where those of other traditions are welcomed. For example, the Paulist Center in Boston—just off the Boston Common—has a Eucharist service each morning at 7:55, timed

---

[21]John Wesley, Sermon 101, "The Duty of Constant Communion," www.whdl.org/duty-constant
-communion-sermon-101.

to give the faithful the option of coming to the Table en route to the office. There is an early morning mass at New York City's Church of Saint Paul the Apostle on the corner of Columbus Avenue and 60th Street that is welcoming to Christians of all traditions. There is a weekday morning Eucharist service at 8:00 at Saint John's Cathedral in Hong Kong.

We come to the Table with the intent that we would cultivate a confidence that Christ is Lord, that Christ Jesus is present, and that the arc of history is long but that in the end, good will triumph. That is, we want to come to the Table as often as possible so that we would know the grace of the words of the psalmist:

> O LORD, my heart is not lifted up,
>   my eyes are not raised too high;
> I do not occupy myself with things
>   too great and too marvelous for me.
> But I have calmed and quieted my soul,
>   like a weaned child with its mother;
>   my soul is like the weaned child that is with me.
> O Israel, hope in the LORD
>   from this time on and forevermore. (Psalm 131)

CONCLUSION

HOSPITALITY, THE GOSPEL, AND LEADERSHIP IN A SECULAR AGE

WHEN WE SPEAK ABOUT WHAT IT MEANS to provide leadership for the church in a secular age, it is imperative that we consider the place of hospitality. Hospitality is a complement and, in many respects, an essential element of all the competencies and capacities discussed in this book. This has always been the case, of course. Hospitality has always been basic to what it means to be the church. But now more than ever, without hospitality, any speaking about the gospel comes up empty. We feel this most keenly in a pluralist, secular society.

We have spoken of the church as a liturgical, catechetical, and missional community, and on all three scores hospitality is the necessary soil in which our worship, teaching, and mission happen. More to the point, it is hospitality that gives each of these a gospel integrity. It is hospitality that is the heartbeat of God toward the church and the world, as well as the heartbeat of the church—both internally to its members and to the world in which the church is located. In the "household of faith" it begins with the "passing of the peace" and the hospitality we show one another in our worship and in our shared lives in community. We welcome one another, as Paul puts it, precisely as Christ welcomed us (Romans 15:7). But it soon also finds expression in the quality of our relationships with our neighbor—those of other religious affiliations and those who have no particular religious commitment. It is hospitality toward each other and toward the world that gives integrity to our worship and our witness.[1]

---

[1] Suggested reading: Joshua W. Jipp, *Saved by Faith and Hospitality* (Grand Rapids, MI: Eerdmans 2017), with foreword by Christine Pohl; Christine Pohl, *Making Room: Recovering Hospitality as*

With respect to our worship—our shared life as a *liturgical* community— radical hospitality to each other marks our common life. Few have spoken so powerfully to this as Dietrich Bonhoeffer in *Life Together*. He reminds us that only through hospitality toward each other are we genuinely the church. This hospitality is marked by listening and attentiveness to the other, but also the ongoing conviction that we accept the other; we do not have an agenda for them other than to let the Spirit do the Spirit's gracious work in the timing of the Spirit.

Hospitality also finds crucial expression in what it means to be a *catechetical* and *missional* community—a teaching-learning community where we intentionally welcome inquirers on a journey of faith, potentially a journey that will take them from a secular worldview where materiality is everything and transcendence nothing to an affective awareness of the love of God which then, in turn, leads to their affirmation that Christ is indeed Lord.

The experience of coming to faith in Christ looks and feels very different in a secular society. As often as not, it is a journey—a series of conversations and experiences by which a person, slowly and gradually, comes to an awareness of the other, the transcendent, including the remarkable wonder that this transcendent other is a benevolent presence and has a name: Father, Son, and Holy Spirit. Because this tends to happen slowly, the genius of congregational life in this regard is twofold: first, that we know the art of hospitality, and second, that we are intentional in our approach to Christian initiation.

But it is essential that we not start with Christian initiation. True hospitality does not have a preconceived agenda; it is not a technique by which people are treated as a means to an end. We eschew an instrumentalist approach to others. It is not, ultimately, about being friendly to someone so they buy the product I am selling or embrace my religion. True hospitality is an end in its own right; it needs no other justification than that this is what it means to be the church.

---

a Christian Tradition (Grand Rapids, MI: Eerdmans, 1999); Bryan Stone, *Evangelism After Pluralism: The Ethics of Christian Witness* (Grand Rapids, MI: Baker Academic, 2018); Matthew Kaemingk, *Christian Hospitality and Muslim Immigration in an Age of Fear* (Grand Rapids, MI: Eerdmans, 2018).

Hospitality is basic Christian practice, but it is a learned art—a *cultivated* capacity. It comes naturally to no one. Think in terms of concentric circles. We begin with our own faith community; in the words of 1 Peter, we are hospitable to one another "without complaining" (1 Peter 4:9). We welcome the other, in community. Then this disposition toward each other necessarily shapes the way we engage the immediate neighborhood and, more, the town and city in which we are located. Here the imperative is that we learn to welcome the other whose politics and religion may be quite foreign to our own.

And then, of course, we welcome the refugee, the immigrant, the stranger. In the end, the true test of our hospitality is whether it is offered with no expectation of return or benefit to the one offering the hospitality. We do it because that is what Christians do. Hospitality is a virtue to which the ancient church calls us, and it is consistent with the prophetic witness. Hospitality is part of the very heart of God and thus one of the hallmarks of the reign of God in our world.

Hospitality is an essential spiritual practice for a world that is marked by diversity, high migration, and political polarization. It is an act of both generosity and justice. Hospitality means that we receive the other, but it also means that we go to the other. We tend to them in *their* place; we receive *their* hospitality. We both give and receive. The boundaries in our lives are permeable—we receive others into our world and we graciously enter into the world of the other. We take a risk with the other; we eat with the other. We learn from and with the other, including our Muslim neighbor. We confront our fears, asking if it makes any sense whatsoever that fear keeps us from embodying the gospel and showing radical hospitality to the other. This is why it is so imperative that we cultivate the interiority by which we live in an anxious world with grace, integrity, courage, and creativity.

ESSENTIAL READING LIST
FOR LEADING THE CHURCH
IN A SECULAR AGE

SECULARITY AND RESPONSES TO SECULARITY

Bowen, Kurt. *Christians in a Secular World: The Canadian Experience.* Montreal: McGill-Queens University Press, 2004.

Bruce, Steve. *Secularization: In Defense of an Unfashionable Theory.* Oxford: Oxford University Press, 2011.

Dobbelaere, Karel. *Secularization: An Analysis at Three Levels.* Brussels: Peter Lang, 2002.

Dupré, Louis. *Transcendent Selfhood: The Loss and Rediscovery of the Inner Life.* New York: Seabury, 1976.

Fitch, David E. *Faithful Presence: Seven Disciplines that Shape the Church for Mission.* Downers Grove, IL: InterVarsity Press, 2016.

Hunter, James Davison. *To Change the World: The Irony, Tragedy, and Possibility of Christianity in the Late Modern World.* Oxford: Oxford University Press, 2010.

Martin, David. *On Secularization: Towards a Revised General Theory.* Aldershot: Ashgate, 2005.

McLeod, Hugh, and Werner Usterof. *The Decline of Christianity in Western Europe, 1750–2000.* Cambridge: Cambridge University Press, 2003.

Murray, Stuart. *Post-Christendom: Church and Mission in a Strange New World.* Carlisle: Paternoster, 2004.

Noll, Mark. "Whatever Happened to Christian Canada?" *Church History* 75:2 (June 2006): 245-74.

Smith, James K. A. *How (Not) to Be Secular: Reading Charles Taylor.* Grand Rapids, MI: Eerdmans, 2004.

———. *Who's Afraid of Postmodernism? Taking Derrida, Lyotard, and Foucault to Church.* Grand Rapids, MI: Baker Academic, 2006.

Taylor, Charles. *A Secular Age.* Cambridge, MA: The Belknap Press of Harvard University Press, 2007.

Thiessen, Joel. *The Meaning of Sunday.* Montreal: McGill-Queens University Press, 2015.

WISDOM FROM 1 PETER AND EXILIC LITERATURE

Achtemeier, Paul. *1 Peter: A Commentary on First Peter*. Hermeneia. Minneapolis: Fortress, 1996.

Beach, Lee. *The Church in Exile: Living in Hope After Christendom*. Downers Grove, IL: IVP Academic, 2015.

Bechtel, Carol M. *Esther*. Interpretation. Louisville, KY: Westminster John Knox, 2002.

Birch, Bruce C., Walter Brueggemann, Terence E. Fretheim, and David L Peterson. *A Theological Introduction to the Old Testament*. 2nd ed. Nashville: Abingdon, 2011.

Brueggemann, Walter. *Cadences of Home: Preaching Among the Exiles*. Louisville, KY: Westminster John Knox, 1997.

———. *Deep Memory, Exuberant Hope*. Minneapolis: Fortress, 2000.

———. *The Prophetic Imagination*. Minneapolis: Fortress, 1978.

Davids, Peter H. *The First Epistle of Peter*. New International Commentary on the New Testament. Grand Rapids, MI: Eerdmans, 1990.

Harink, Douglas. *1 & 2 Peter*. Brazos Theological Commentary on the Bible. Grand Rapids, MI: Brazos Press, 2009.

Provan, Iain, V. Philips Long, and Tremper Longman III. *A Biblical History of Israel*. Rev. ed. Louisville, KY: Westminster John Knox, 2015.

Smith-Christopher, Daniel. *A Biblical Theology of Exile*. Minneapolis, Fortress, 2002.

WISDOM FROM THE EARLY CHURCH

Ambrose of Milan. *On the Holy Spirit*. In *St. Ambrose: Select Works and Letters*. Translated by H. de Romestin, E. de Romestin, and H. T. F. Duckworth. Nicene and Post-Nicene Fathers, Second Series, 10. Buffalo, NY: Christian Literature Company, 1896.

Augustine. *The City of God*. Translated by Marcus Dods. Nicene and Post-Nicene Fathers, First Series, 2. Buffalo, NY: Christian Literature Company, 1887. See especially book XIX.

———. *Confessions*. Translated by John K. Ryan. New York: Doubleday, 1960.

Bremmer, Jan N. *The Rise of Christianity Through the Eyes of Gibbon, Harnack and Rodney Stark*. Groningen: Barkhuis, 2010.

Castelli, Elizabeth A. *Martyrdom and Memory: Early Christian Culture Making*. New York: Columbia University Press, 2004.

Coakley, Sarah, ed. *Re-Thinking Gregory of Nyssa*. Malden, MA: Blackwell, 2003.

Dujarier, Michel. *A History of the Catechumenate: The First Six Centuries*. New York: Sadlier, 1979.

Gama, Michael Paul, *Theosis: Patristic Remedy for Evangelical Yearning at the Close of the Modern Age*. Eugene, OR: Wipf & Stock, 2017.

Ford, David. *Wisdom for Today From the Early Church: A Foundational Study*. Waymart, PA: St. Tikhon's Monastery Press, 2014.

Hippolytus. *On the Apostolic Tradition*. Translated by Alistair Stewart-Sykes. Crestwood, NY: St. Vladimir's Seminary Press, 2001.

Kreider, Alan. *The Change of Conversion and the Origin of Christendom*. Eugene, OR: Wipf & Stock, 1999.

Miloski, Gordon. *Baptism and Christian Identity: Teaching in the Triune Name*. Grand Rapids, MI: Eerdmans, 2009.

Sittser, Gerald. "The Catechumenate and the Rise of Christianity." *Journal of Spiritual Formation and Soul Care* 6.2 (Nov 2013): 179-203.

Smith, James K. A. *Awaiting the King: Reforming Public Theology*. Grand Rapids, MI: Baker Academic, 2017.

———. *On the Road with Saint Augustine: A Real-World Spirituality for Restless Hearts*. Grand Rapids, MI: Brazos Press, 2019.

Webber, Robert. *Journey to Jesus: The Worship, Evangelism, and Nurture Mission of the Church*. Nashville: Abingdon, 2001.

PERSPECTIVES FROM HISTORIC MINORITY CHURCHES

Fernando, Ajith. *Sharing the Truth in Love: How to Relate to People of Other Faiths*. Grand Rapids, MI: Discovery House, 2014.

Kim, Sebastian C. H. *Christian Theology in Asia*. Cambridge: Cambridge University Press, 2008.

Kitamori, Kazoh. *The Theology of the Pain of God*. Richmond, VA: John Knox Press, 1965.

Koyama, Kosuke. *No Handle on the Cross: An Asian Meditation on the Crucified Mind*. Maryknoll, NY: Orbis Books, 1976.

———. *Waterbuffalo Theology*. Maryknoll, NY: Orbis Books, 1974.

Song, C. S. *Tell Us Our Names: Story Theology from an Asian Perspective*. Maryknoll, NY: Orbis Books, 1984.

———. *Third-Eye Theology*, rev. ed. Maryknoll, NY: Orbis Books, 1991.

Stephanous, Andrea Zaki. *Political Islam, Citizenship, and Minorities: The Future of Arab Christians in the Islamic Middle East*. Lanham, MD: University Press of America, 2010.

WISDOM FROM THE EUROPEAN EXPERIENCE

Backhouse, Stephen. *Kierkegaard: A Single Life*. Grand Rapids, MI: Zondervan, 2016.

Bonhoeffer, Dietrich. *Ethics*. Translated by Reinhard Krauss, Charles C. West, and Douglas W. Stott. Dietrich Bonhoeffer Works 6. Minneapolis: Fortress, 2008.

———. *Letters and Papers from Prison*. Translated by Isabel Best, Lisa E. Dahill, Reinhard Krauss, Nancy Lukens, Barbara Rumscheidt, Martin Rumscheidt, and Douglas W. Stott. Dietrich Bonhoeffer Works 8. Minneapolis: Fortress, 2010.

———. *Life Together and Prayer Book of the Bible*. Translated by Daniel W. Bloesch and James H. Burtness. Dietrich Bonhoeffer Works 5. Minneapolis: Fortress, 1996.

Ellul, Jacques. *The Politics of God and the Politics of Man*. Translated by Geoffrey W. Bromiley. Grand Rapids, MI: Eerdmans, 1972.

———. *Presence in the Modern World.* Translated by Lisa Richmond. Eugene, OR: Cascade, 2016.

———. *The Subversion of Christianity.* Translated by Geoffrey W. Bromiley. Grand Rapids, MI: Eerdmans, 1986.

Kierkegaard, Søren. *The Present Age: On the Death of Rebellion.* New York: Harper Perennial, 2010. See also *Either/Or, Fear and Trembling, Purity of Heart Is to Will One Thing,* and *Training in Christianity.*

Newbigin, Lesslie. *Foolishness to the Greeks: The Gospel and Western Culture.* Grand Rapids, MI: Eerdmans, 1986.

———. *The Gospel in a Pluralist Society.* Grand Rapids, MI: Eerdmans, 1989.

———. *The Household of God: Lectures on the Nature of the Church.* London: SCM Press, 1953.

———. *Proper Confidence: Faith, Doubt, and Certainty in Christian Discipleship.* Grand Rapids, MI: Eerdmans, 1995.

THE PRACTICE OF LEADERSHIP: LITURGICAL, CATECHETICAL, MISSIONAL, AND ECUMENICAL

Berger, Timothy. *The Juvenilization of American Christianity.* Grand Rapids, MI: Eerdmans, 2012.

Cavanaugh, William T. *Field Hospital: The Church's Engagement with a Wounded World.* Grand Rapids, MI: Eerdmans, 2015.

Chan, Simon. *Liturgical Theology: The Church as a Worshipping Community.* Downers Grove, IL: IVP Academic, 2006.

Davis, John Jefferson. *Worship and the Reality of God: An Evangelical Theology of Real Presence.* Downers Grove, IL: IVP Academic, 2010.

Dykstra, Craig. *Growing in the Life of Faith: Education and Christian Practices,* 2nd ed. Louisville, KY: Westminster John Knox, 2005.

Garrido, Ann. *Redeeming Conflict: 12 Habits for Christian Leaders.* Notre Dame, IN: Ave Maria Press, 2016.

Gross, Bobby. *Living the Christian Year: Time to Inhabit the Story of God.* Downers Grove, IL: InterVarsity Press, 2009.

Hold, Kendra G., and Matthew T. Matthews. *Shaping the Christian Life: Worship and the Religious Affections.* Louisville, KY: Westminster John Knox, 2006.

Inazu, John D. *Confident Pluralism: Surviving and Thriving through Deep Difference* Chicago: University of Chicago Press, 2016.

Kim, Grace Ji-Sun, and Graham Hill. *Healing Our Broken Humanity: Practices for Revitalizing the Church and Renewing the World.* Downers Grove, IL: InterVarsity Press, 2018.

Nelson, Tom. *The Economics of Neighborly Love: Investing in Your Community's Compassion and Capacity.* Downers Grove, IL: InterVarsity Press, 2017.

Ryan, Thomas. *Christian Unity: How You Can Make a Difference.* New York: Paulist Press, 2015.

Paas, Stefan. *Church Planting in the Secular West: Learning from the European Experience.* Grand Rapids, MI: Eerdmans, 2016.

Scott, Susan. *Difficult Conversations: How to Discuss What Matters Most.* New York: Penguin Books, 2010.

Smith, James K. A. *Imagining the Kingdom: How Worship Works.* Grand Rapids, MI: Baker Academic, 2013.

Taylor, W. David O. *For the Beauty of the Church: Casting a Vision for the Arts.* Grand Rapids, MI: Baker Books, 2010.

Webber, Robert E. *Ancient-Future Worship: Proclaiming and Enacting God's Narrative.* Grand Rapids, MI: Baker Books, 2008.

Whitlock, Luder G., Jr. *Divided We Fall: Overcoming a History of Christian Disunity.* Phillipsburg, NJ: P&R, 2017.

SPIRITUAL PRACTICE FOR A SECULAR AGE

Dupré, Louis. "Seeking Christian Interiority: An Interview with Louis Dupré," *The Christian Century*, July 16-23, 1997, 654-60. www.religion-online.org/article/seeking-christian-interiority-an-interview-with-louis-dupr.

Ford, David F. *The Shape of Living: Spiritual Directions for Everyday Life.* Grand Rapids, MI: Zondervan, 1997.

Friedman, Edwin. *Generation to Generation: Family Process in Church and Synagogue.* New York: Guilford, 2011.

Lane, Belden C., *The Solace of Fierce Landscapes: Exploring Desert and Mountain Spirituality.* New York: Oxford University Press, 1998.

Merton, Thomas. *New Seeds of Contemplation.* London: Burns and Oates, 1962.

Schmemann, Alexander. *For the Life of the World: Sacraments and Orthodoxy.* Crestwood, NY: St. Vladimir's Seminary Press, 1998. First published in 1963.

Smith, Gordon T. *Teach Us to Pray.* Downers Grove, IL: InterVarsity Press, 2018.

Williams, Rowan. *The Truce of God.* Grand Rapids, MI: Eerdmans, 1983.

NAME AND SUBJECT INDEX

Accad, Martin, 67-68, 148

Achtemeier, Paul, 44

Agang, Sunday Bobai, 68

Algeria, 75-76

Ambrose of Milan, 32, 50-51
  and the catechumenate, 55-58
  and political influence, 50-51, 54, 105, 142, 144
  trinitarian preaching and hymns, 60-64, 120

Anglican Church, 116, 157, 175

Arab Baptist Theological Seminary, 148

Arianism, 50-51, 60

Auden, W. H., 165

Augustine of Hippo, 15, 32, 50-54, 88, 101, 120
  and the catechumenate, 55-58
  and *City of God*, 51-54
  conversion narrative, 56-57
  and interior life, 58-62
  and political influence, 51-55
  on the Trinity, 64

Balthasar, Hans Urs von, 167

Barth, Karl, 80, 86, 156, 166

Baum, Gregory, 16-17

Beach, Lee, 37

Bechtel, Carol, 37

Bell, George, 156-57

Benedict of Nursia, 53, 58, 101

Berger, Peter, 13

Berman, Morris, 26

Bethge, Eberhard, 82

Bibi, Asia, 75

Bonhoeffer, Dietrich, 81-87, 96, 102, 142, 178
  and ecumenism, 154-57, 159, 161

Boyd, Greg, 29

Brown, Callum G., 9

Brooks, David, 103-4

Bruce, Steve, 13

Brueggemann, Walter, 37, 41-43, 129, 166

Buchanan, Mark, 174

Buddhism, 67, 69, 169

Cahill, Thomas, 26

Calvin, John, 123, 161, 175

Canada, 7, 8-12, 13, 14, 29, 107

Carter, Jimmy, 29

catechumenate
  early Christian, 55-58
  and 1 Peter, 132-37
  restoring the ancient, 128-32

Catholic Church. *See* Roman Catholic Church

Cavanaugh, William T., 115

Chan, Simon, 129

Chesterton, G. K., 80

China, 32, 66-67, 71, 76-78

Christian and Missionary Alliance, 116

Christianity Today, 68, 105

Chrysostom, John, 49

church calendar, 108, 121, 130, 133-34

Coakley, Sarah, 64, 81

Confessions (Augustine), 15, 56, 59, 60-62, 64

Constantine, 49

Constantineanu, Corneliu, 73-74

Cox, Daniel, 11

Czech Republic, 81, 124

Das, R. C., 69

Dickinson, Emily, 151

Dobbelaere, Karel, 12-13

Dominic, Saint, 102

Dreher, Rod, 26-27, 101-2

Dupré, Louis, 15-16, 58-59, 168

Dykstra, Craig, 127

Dylan, Bob, 1

Eisenhower, Dwight, 144

Ellul, Jacques, 81, 87-93, 96, 101, 105, 142

Emerson, Michael O., 108

Endo, Shusaku, 75

Eucharist. *See* Lord's Supper

Fach, Terry, 121

fear, 41, 47-48, 74, 103, 137, 141, 164-68

Fernando, Ajith, 68

First Amendment, 11

First Nations (Canada), 107

Fitch, David E, 30-31

FitzGerald, Frances, 28-29
Ford, Coleman, 62
Ford, David, 170
Francis, Saint, 102
Friedman, Edwin H., 166-67
Galli, Mark, 105
Gama, Michael Paul, 64
Garrido, Ann, 146
Germany, 80, 81, 83-86, 154, 156-57
Graham, Billy, 144
Graham, Franklin, 29, 144
Great Britain/England, 9, 14, 49, 80, 156
Gregory of Nyssa, 49, 65
Gregory the Great, 49
Gross, Bobby, 121
Haizi, 71-72, 111
Halík, Tomáš, 81, 124
Harink, Douglas, 44, 46-47, 135
Herbert, George, 19
Herriot, Trevor, 174
Hill, Graham, 115-16
Hindmarsh, Bruce, 33
hope, 41-43, 92-93, 123, 142
hospitality, 125-26, 135, 177-79
Hunter, James Davison, 30-31
Inazu, John, 106
Irenaeus, 49
Isaac, Munther, 78-79
Islam/Muslims, 28, 68-69, 73, 75-76, 106, 148
Jackson, J. Scott, 77
Japan, 66, 78
Jesuits, 52, 103
Jenkins, Philip, 76
Jipp, Joshua W., 177
Kaemingk, Matthew, 178
Kennedy, John F., 144
Kierkegaard, Søren, 80, 102, 165, 170
Kim, Grace Ji-Sun, 115-16
Kitamori, Kazoh, 78
Knowles, David, 26
Lane, Belden C., 174
Lebanon, 66, 67-68, 148-49
Liao Yiwu, 76
Lomagio, Shapri D., 106
Lord's Supper/Eucharist, 121, 122-23, 126, 158, 174-76
Luther, Martin, 123
Marsh, Charles, 154-56
Martin, David, 13-14
Merton, Thomas, 124
Meyerson, Debra E., 149-51
Miloski, Gordon, 65

Mitchell, George J., 146
Moberg, David, 29
Moltmann, Jürgen, 80
Moore, Roy, 105
Morris, Thomas H., 130
Muslim. *See* Islam
Native Americans, 107
Nelson, Tom, 145
New Zealand, 8, 12, 14, 107
Newbigin, Lesslie, 93-96, 107, 109, 112, 140, 145
Niebuhr, H. Richard, 22-23
Nigeria, 68
Nixon, Richard, 29, 144
Nouwen, Henri, 165
Origen of Alexandria, 49
Paas, Stefan, 160-61
Pakistan, 75
Palmer, Parker, 165
Panikkar, Raimon, 69
Paulists, 103
peacemaking and conflict resolution, 146-49
pluralism, 7-8, 68, 93, 95, 106, 110-11, 143
Pohl, Christine, 177
political engagement, 142-46
prayer, 86, 93, 163, 170-72
Presbyterian Church, 116
Provan, Iain, 35
Quebec, 9-10
Rahner, Karl, 59, 168
Republican Party, 11, 29
Reynolds, Thomas E., 110-11
Rite of Christian Initiation of Adults (RCIA), 130
Roman Catholic Church, 14, 84, 130, 155-57
Romero, Oscar, 77
Rule of Saint Benedict, 156, 170
Ryan, Thomas, 159, 160
sabbath observance, 173
Sabellianism, 61
Scott, Susan, 146
Scully, Maureen A., 149-51
secularism, 8, 24, 70, 100, 110-11
secularity, 7-20, 25-32, 68-71, 100, 104, 110-11
Schmemann, Alexander, 100, 119, 162
Sider, Ron, 29
Sittser, Gerald, 57-58, 129
Smith, Christian, 108
Smith, James K. A., 15, 17-19, 54-55, 101-2, 108-9, 119
Smith-Christopher, Daniel, 36-37
Song, C. S., 69
spiritual direction, 172-73

Stark, Rodney, 13, 58
Stephanous, Andrea Z., 73
Stone, Bryan, 178
Sudharkar, Paul, 69
Taylor, Charles, 15, 17-19
Taylor, David O., 124
Tertullian, 22, 49
Theodosius, 49, 51
Thiessen, Joel, 12-13
Tiananmen Square, 71, 77-78
Tolstoy, Leo, 167
Trump, Donald, 29, 144
Truth and Reconciliation Commission
  (Canada), 107

United Kingdom. *See* Great Britain
United States, 8-12, 14, 27, 50, 107
Vanderklippe, Nathan, 77-78
walking as spiritual practice, 174
Wallis, Jim, 29
Weil, Simone, 19
Wesley, John, 62, 123, 175
Whitlock, Luder G., Jr., 159
Williams, Rowan, 81, 109-10, 124, 165-66,
  171
Wolterstorff, Nicholas, 107
Wright, N. T., 18
Yang Xiaoli, 71-72
Zhang Yinxian, 76

SCRIPTURE INDEX

OLD TESTAMENT

2 Chronicles
36:23-24, *35*

Ezra
7, *36*
7:27, *36*

Nehemiah
9:36-37, *35*
13, *36*

Psalms
131, *176*

Proverbs
15:23, *43*

Isaiah
43:1-5, *48*
58, *40, 107, 117*
58:6-8, *40*

Jeremiah
28, *43*
29, *36, 54*
29:1-7, *47*
29:7, *36, 139*
40–43, *35*

Lamentations
1:1, *35*

Ezekiel
1:1-3, *38*
16:46-48, *39*

Daniel
3, *78*

NEW TESTAMENT

Matthew
28, *170*
28:10, *170*
28:20, *127, 170*

John
15:4, *168, 169*
15:7, *134*

Acts
2:42, *122, 127*
20:7, *175*

Romans
8:17, *78, 133*
13:13-14, *57*
15:7, *177*

Galatians
6:9-10, *163*

Ephesians
4:15, *127*

Philippians
4, *172*
4:8, *172*

Colossians
1:27, *170*
1:28-29, *127*
3:1-3, *169*
3:2, *122*
3:16, *134*
4:5-6, *145*

2 Timothy
2:2, *128*

Hebrews
5:12, *128*

1 Peter
1:3, *122*
1:3-12, *132*
1:8, *132*
1:11, *45*
1:13, *134*
1:14, *45*
1:17, *44*
1:18, *133*
1:21, *133*
1:22, *135*
1:23, *134*
1:25, *134*
2:2, *134, 136*
2:9, *132*
2:11, *44, 132*
2:11-12, *45*
2:11–4:11, *44*
2:13, *45*
2:13–3:7, *45*
2:17, *45*
2:23, *46*
2:24, *133*
3:8, *135*
3:14, *137*
3:15, *46*
3:15-16, *145*
3:16, *46*
3:18-19, *133*
3:18-22, *133*
4:8, *135*
4:9, *135, 179*
4:10, *135*
4:12, *45*
4:13, *133*
4:19, *46*
5, *172*
5:1-5, *135*
5:6-7, *137*
5:7, *48*
5:12, *137*